French - Hindi

LEARNING FLASHCARDS

FOR BABIES TODDLERS

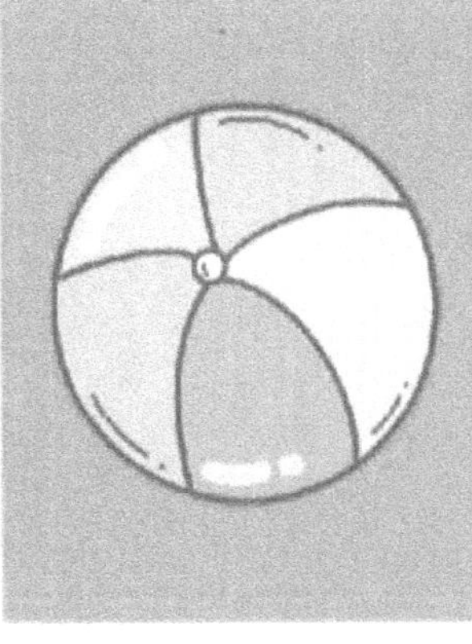

alligator

मगर

The alligator is having a party.

fourmi

चींटी

The ant is red.

ours

भालू

The bear loves you.

abeille

मधुमक्खी

The bee is saying hello.

oiseau

चिड़िया

The bird is flying.

papillon

तितली

The butterfly is pretty.

chameau

ऊंट

The camel has a hump.

chat

बिल्ली

The cat is happy.

dinosaure

डायनासोर

The dinosaur is laying eggs.

poulet

मुर्गी

The chicken is dancing.

vache

गाय

The cow has a bell.

cerf

हिरन

The reindeer has a toy.

chien

कुत्ता

The dog has two floppy ears.

dauphin

डॉल्फिन

The dolphin is swimming.

canard

बत्तख

The duck has a bow.

aigle

ईगल

The eagle is looking for food.

l'éléphant

हाथी

The elephant is sitting.

poisson

मछली

The fish is a clownfish.

libellule

ड्रैगनफ्लाई

The dragonfly is blue.

renard

लोमड़ी

The fox has a red nose.

grenouille

मेढक

The frog is smiling.

girafe

जिराफ़

The giraffe has a long neck.

chèvre

बकरा

The goat has a beard

ver de terre

कीड़ा

The worm is in the apple

poule

मुर्गी

The hen has chicks.

hippopotame

जलहस्ती

The hippo is big.

cheval

घोड़ा

The horse is fast.

kangourou

कंगेरू

The kangaroo has a baby.

chaton

बिल्ली का बच्चा

The kitten is playing.

lion

सिंह

The lion has a mane.

homard

झींगा मछली

The lobster is red.

singe

बंदर

The monkey has a tail.

poulpe

ऑक्टोपस

The octopus has food.

hibou

उल्लू

The owls have big eyes.

panda

पांडा

The panda wears a diaper.

porc

सूअर

The pig is fat and pink.

chiot

कुत्ते का बच्चा

The dog is brown.

lapin

खरगोश

The rabbit has a carrot.

rat

चूहा

The mouse is writing something.

crabe

केकड़ा

The crab has two pinchers.

requin

शार्क

The shark is scary.

mouton

भेड़

The sheep are very fluffy.

escargot

घोंघा

The snail is slow.

serpent

साँप

The snake has poison.

araignée

मकड़ी

The spider is purple.

écureuil

गिलहरी

The squirrel has a nut.

tigre

बाघ

The tiger has a red bow.

tortue

कछुआ

The turtle has a shell.

loup

भेड़िया

The wolf is smiling.

zèbre

ज़ेबरा

The zebra is black and white.

dinde

तुर्की

The turkey has two legs.

coq

मुर्गा

The rooster will crow.

perroquet

तोता

The parrot is colorful.

hérisson

कांटेदार जंगली चूहा

The hedgehog has apples.

pomme

सेब

The apple has a leaf.

abricot

खुबानी

The apricot is yellow.

avocat

एवोकाडो

The avocado has a nut.

banane

केला

The banana is yellow.

la mûre

ब्लैकबेरी

There are a lot of blackberries.

cassis

blackcurrant

The blackcurrants are yummy.

myrtille

ब्लूबेरी

The blueberries are sweet.

cerise

चेरी

The cherries have a stem.

noix de coco

नारियल

The coconuts have juice.

figues

अंजीर

The fig has seeds.

grain de raisin

अंगूर

The grapes are purple.

pamplemousse

चकोतरा

The grapefruits are sour.

kiwi

कीवी

The kiwi is fresh.

citron

नींबू

The lemons are yellow.

citron vert

चूना

We have lots of lime.

litchi

लीची

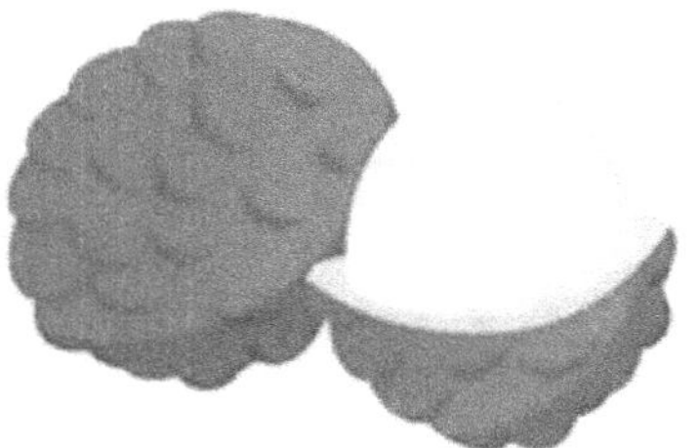

I like to eat lychee.

mandarine

मंडारिन संतरे

Oranges are refreshing.

mangue

आम

Mango is my favorite fruit.

orange

संतरा

Mandarins are like oranges.

papaye

पपीता

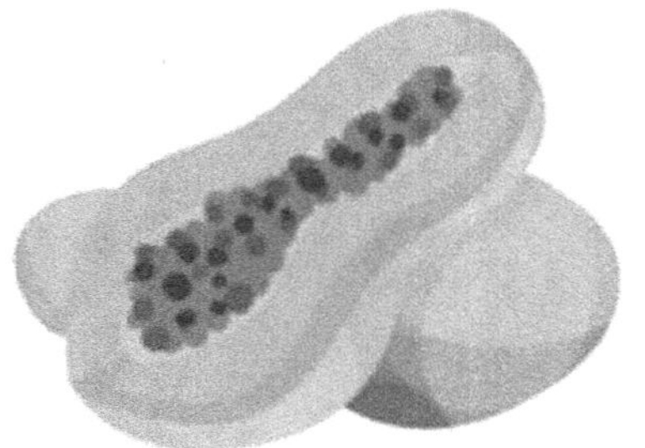

Papayas have lots of seeds.

pêche

आड़ू

Peaches are juicy.

poire

नाशपाती

Pears have a strange figure.

ananas

अनानास

The pineapple has a thumbs up.

prune

बेर

Plums are healthy for you.

grenade

अनार

Pomegranates are all red.

framboise

रसभरी

The raspberry is shiny.

fraise

स्ट्रॉबेरी

The strawberry has leaves on top.

pastèque

तरबूज

The watermelon is big.

mandarine

संतरा

The tangerine looks like an orange.

tarte

पाई

I like to eat apple pie.

gâteau

केक

That cake is huge.

bonbons

कैंडी

Candy is not good for your teeth.

biscuit

कुकी

Cookies are easy to make.

donut

डोनट

I like strawberry donuts.

crème glacée

आइसक्रीम

The ice cream is melting.

muffin

टिकिया

The muffin has a cute wrapper.

pudding

पुडिंग

We eat pudding on Christmas.

classeur

जिल्दसाज़

I keep pictures in my binder.

livre

पुस्तक

I like to eat books.

sac à dos

बैग

The backpack has lots of stuff.

les ciseaux

कैंची

I have scissors in my bag.

épingles

पिंस

Pins can hold stuff up.

agrafe

क्लिप

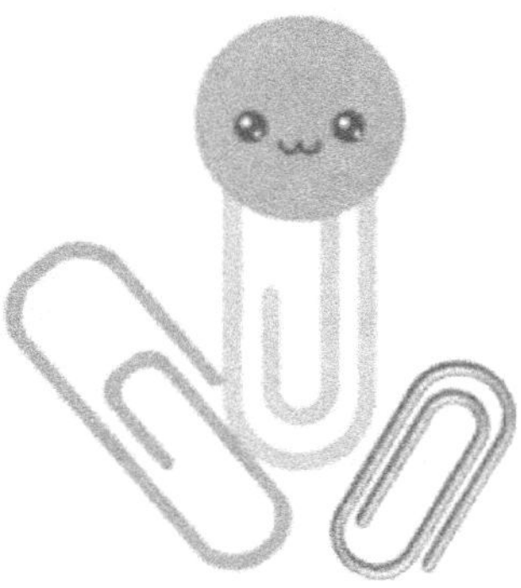

Clips can hold up paper.

papier

कागज़

I have lots of paper.

agrafeuse

ऊन बेचनेवाला

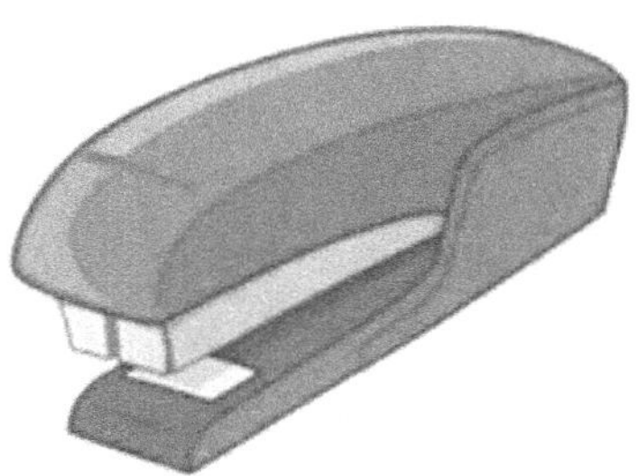

My stapler is shiny and red.

calculatrice

कैलकुलेटर

My calculator has buttons.

règle

शासक

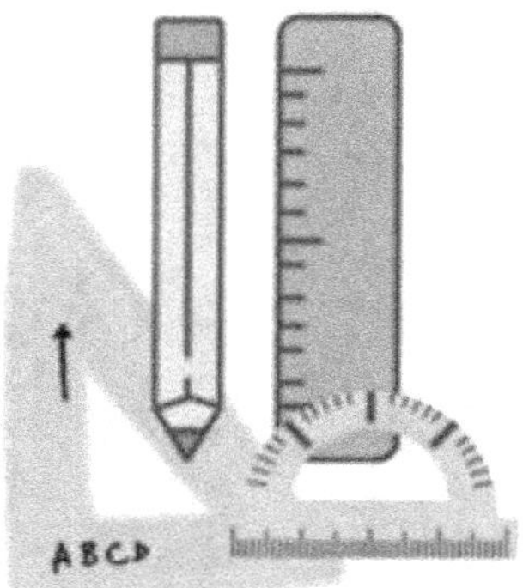

I have lots of rulers.

la colle

गोंद

The glue is sticky.

bibliothèque

किताबों की अलमारी

My bookcase has lots of things.

calendrier

पंचांग

I have a calendar on my table.

chaise

कुरसी

My chair is fancy.

l'horloge

घड़ी

The clock says that it's 3 o'clock.

ordinateur

संगणक

I do things on my computer.

bureaux

डेस्क

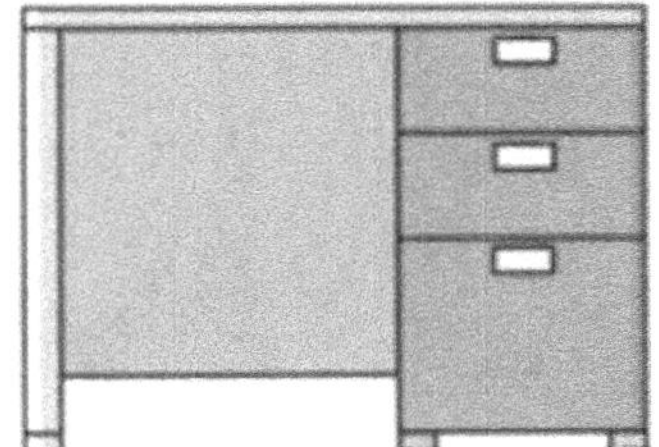

I put lots of things on my desk.

dictionnaire

शब्दकोश

The dictionary has lots of words.

la gomme

रबड़

Erasers are used with pencils.

carte

नक्शा

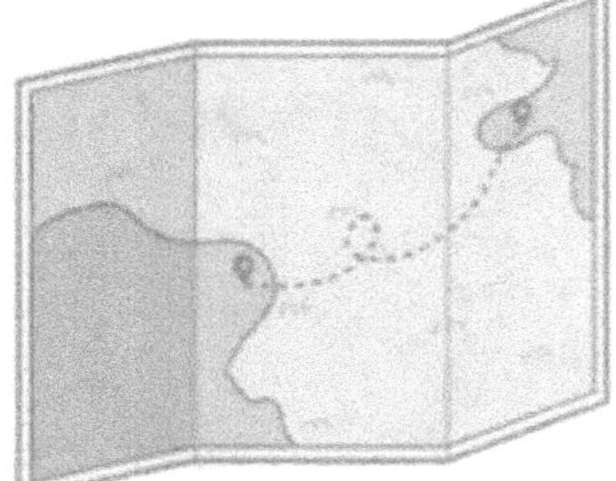

The map shows you different places.

carnet

स्मरण पुस्तक

I use notebooks at school.

stylo

कलम

My pen is very pretty.

crayon

पेंसिल

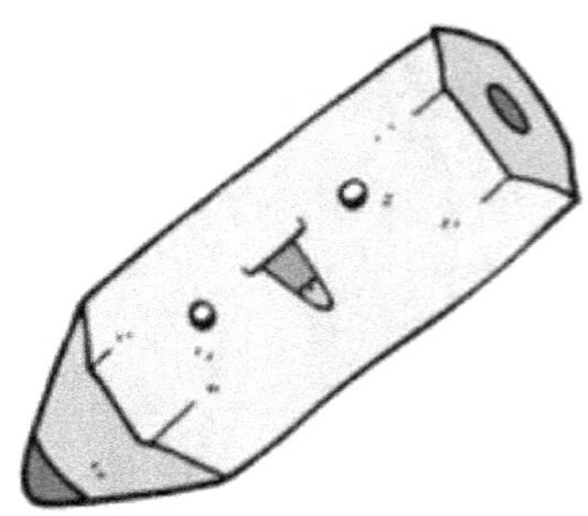

My friend gave me a pencil.

ceinture

बेल्ट

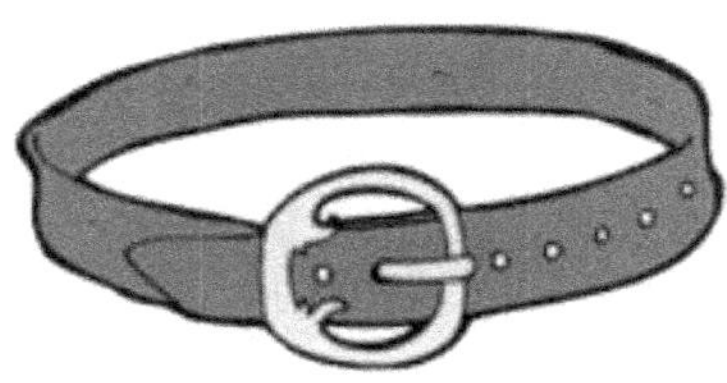

I have a belt on my pants.

bottes

जूते

I have big brown boots.

chapeau

टोपी

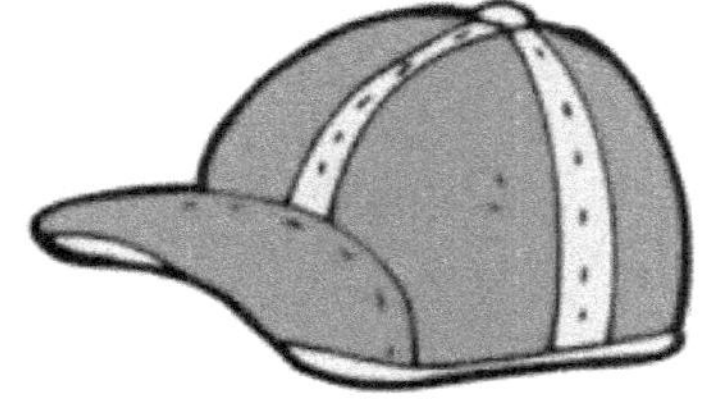

My mom bought me a new cap.

manteau

कोट

She has a long yellow coat.

robes

कपड़े

My dress has a bow.

gants

दस्ताने

I got new gloves.

chapeau

टोपी

That hat is for a wicked witch.

veste

जैकेट

The jacket is cozy.

jeans

जीन्स

My jeans are long.

pyjamas

पाजामा

I sleep in my pajamas.

un pantalon

पैंट

The bear is wearing pants.

imperméable

रेनकोट

We wear our raincoats when it is raining.

écharpe

दुपट्टा

The baby has a scarf around his neck.

chemise

कमीज

I like this shirt the best.

des chaussures

जूते

I have red and blue shoes.

jupe

स्कर्ट

My skirt has lots of buttons.

pantalon

ढीला पतलून

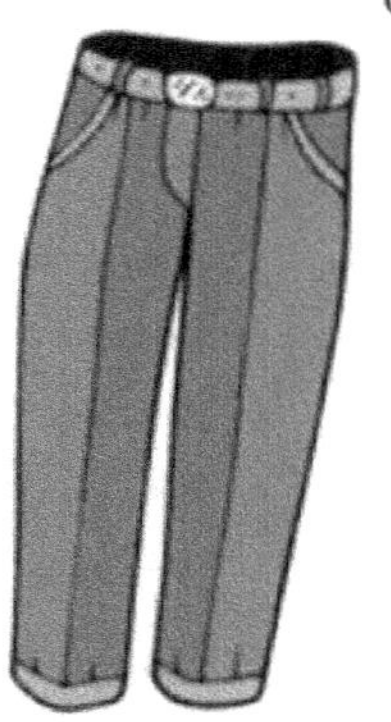

My dad wears slacks.

chaussons

चप्पलें

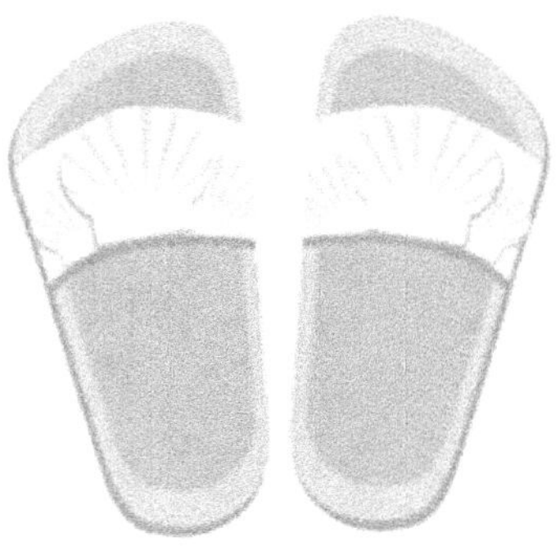

I have seashells on my sandals.

chaussettes

मोज़े

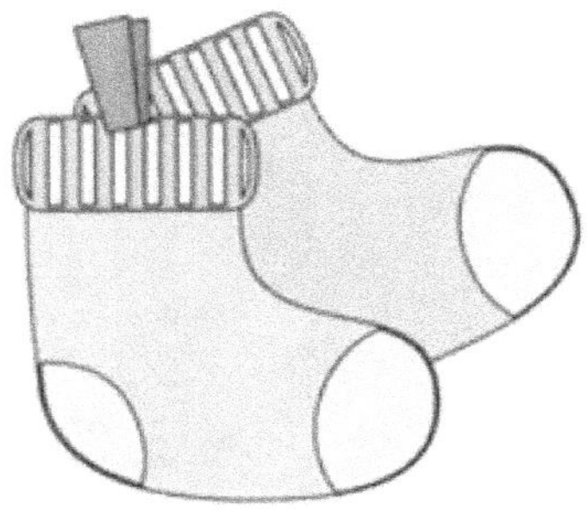

My baby sister wears socks.

costume

सूट

My brother is wearing a suit.

chandail

स्वेटर

I am wearing a sweater for winter.

cravate

नेकटाई

My dad wears a tie to meetings.

pantalon

पतलून

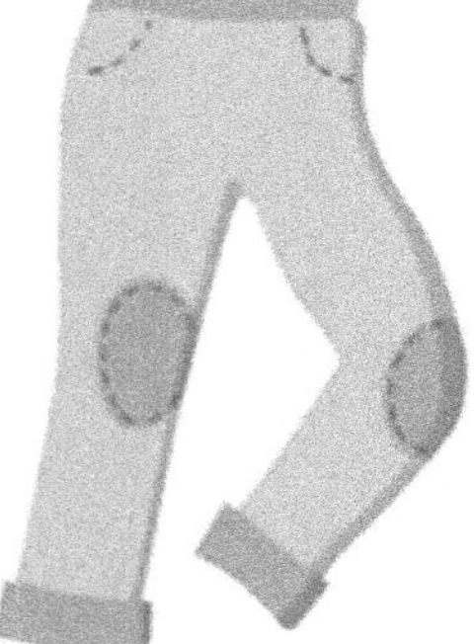

The trousers look like jeans.

slip

जांघिया

I always wear my underwear.

maillot de corps

नीचे का कपड़ा

My undershirt has a star.

une

एक

Number one and the bee are friends.

deux

दो

The cat and the mouse both love two.

trois

तीन

The bear gives number three a present.

quatre

चार

Number four is a home for the cat.

cinq

पांच

Number five hatches an egg.

six

छह

Number six is going to eat a carrot.

sept

सात

Number seven is playing with the tiger.

huit

आठ

Number eight is funny.

neuf

नौ

Number nine meets the parrot.

dix

दस

Number ten is smiling.

onze

ग्यारह

Number eleven has big eyes.

douze

बारह

Number twelve is number one and two.

treize

तेरह

Number thirteen is excited.

quatorze

चौदह

The number fourteen is vast.

quinze

पंद्रह

The number fifteen is green.

seize

सोलह

Sixteen is my lucky number.

dix-sept

सत्रह

Number seventeen look alike.

dix-huit

अठारह

Number eighteen will go to the circus.

dix-neuf

उन्नीस

I am nineteen now!

vingt

बीस

Number twenty has a zero.

fourmi

चींटी

The ant has lots of legs.

cloche

घंटी

The bell will ring.

vache

गाय

The cow has a bow.

poupée
गुड़िया
D
She has a cute bear doll.

oeuf
अंडा
E
The chick has hatched out of the egg.

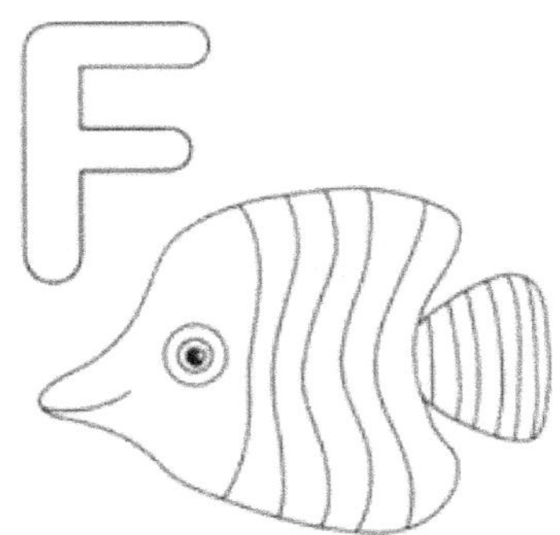

poisson
मछली
F
The fish is swimming in the water.

chèvre
बकरा
G
The goat is sitting on the grass.

chapeau
टोपी
H
He is wearing a hat.

crème glacée
आइसक्रीम
I
I like to eat ice cream.

confiture

जाम

The kitten is sitting on the jam jar.

chaton

बिल्ली का बच्चा

The cat is sleeping on the floor.

lion

सिंह

The lion is waiting for the tiger.

rat

चूहा

The mouse has lots of presents.

nez

नाक

The reindeer has a red nose.

hibou

उल्लू

The owl is sleeping.

porc

सूअर

The pig will eat cupcakes.

reine

रानी

The queen has a big crown.

lapin

खरगोश

The rabbit is jumping up and down.

mouton

भेड़

The sheep have fluffy wool.

tortue

कछुआ

The turtle has a shell.

parapluie

छतरी

The mouse is holding an umbrella.

van

वैन

The van is driving along the road.

pastèque

तरबूज

The watermelon has lots of seeds.

xylophone

सिलाफ़न

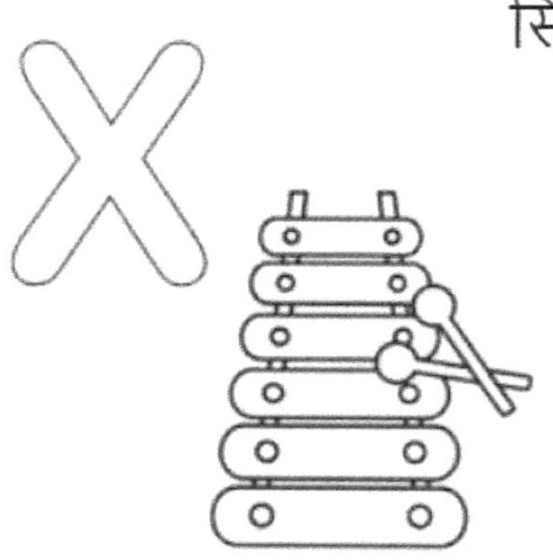

We are going to play the xylophone.

yaourt

दही

We opened the yogurt can.

zèbre

ज़ेबरा

The zebra is surprised.

rose

गुलाबी

Most of my clothes are pink.

marron

भूरा

color the word and
the picture in pink

brown

My chocolate is brown.

gris

धूसर

color the word and
the picture in pink

gray

I don't like the color gray.

vert

हरा

color the word and
the picture in pink

green

The vegetables are green.

jaune

पीला

color the word and
the picture in pink

yellow

Bananas are yellow.

blanc

सफेद

color the word and
the picture in pink

white

The paper that I write on is white.

rouge

लाल

color the word and
the picture in pink

red

Apples are red.

bleu

नीला

color the word and
the picture in pink

The night sky is blue.

percer

ड्रिल

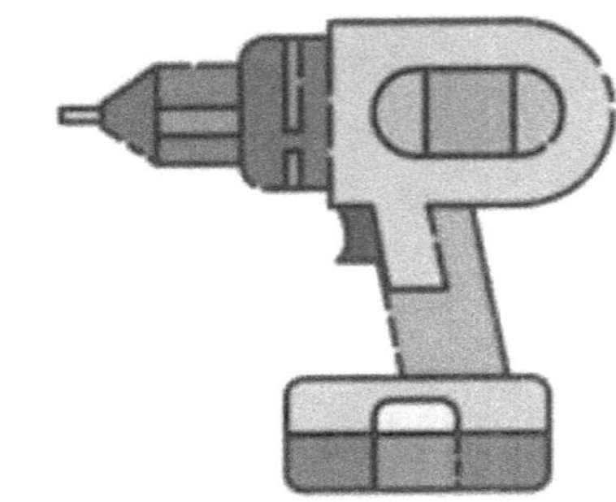

The drill will help us fix this.

marteau

हथौड़ा

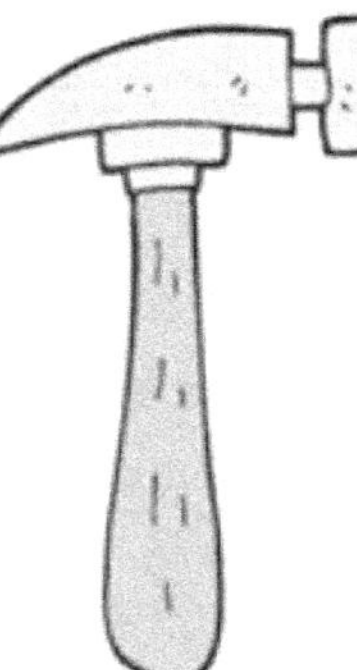

The hammer is going to nail the picture.

couteau

चाकू

The knife is sharp.

pinces

चिमटा

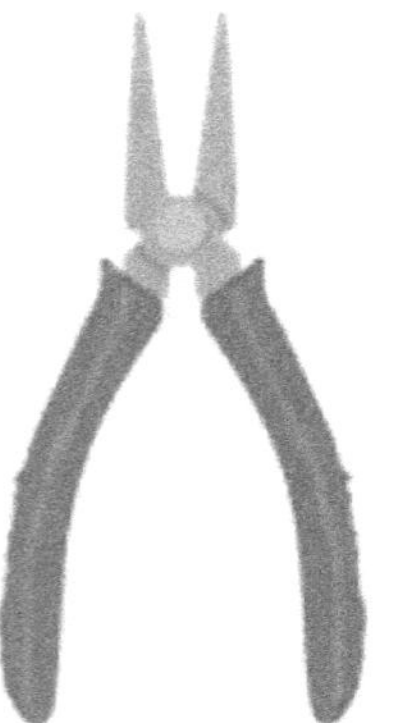

The plier is used for many things.

vu

देखा

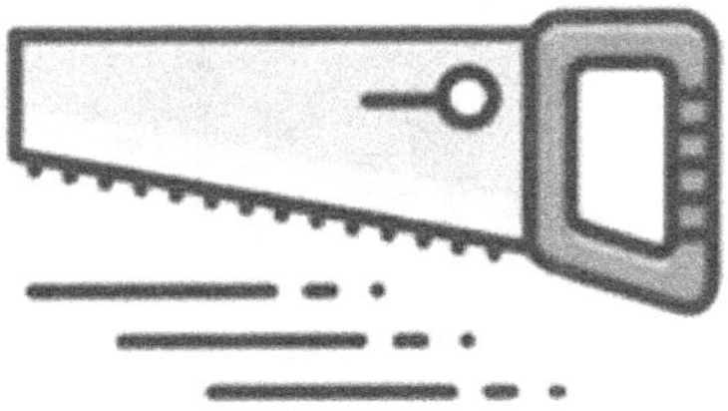

The saw can chop wood.

les ciseaux

कैंची

I use scissors to cut paper.

tournevis

पेंचकस

The screwdriver can screw in the knots.

clé

पाना

The wrench can help unscrew the knots.

avion

विमान

The airplane is going to leave now.

vélo

साइकिल

The bicycle is beautiful.

bateau

नाव

The boat is floating on the water.

autobus

बस

The bus is going to school.

voiture

गाड़ी

The car is green.

hélicoptère

हेलीकॉप्टर

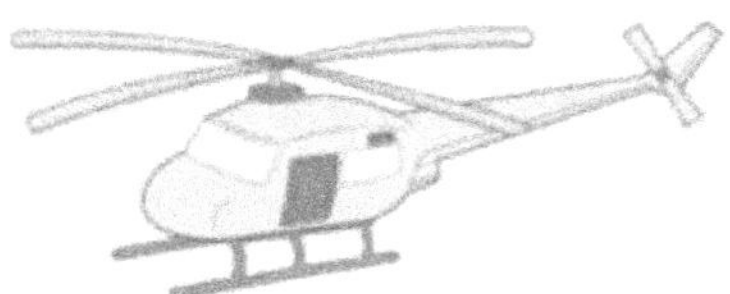

The helicopter is looking for something.

cheval

घोड़ा

You can ride the horse.

jet

जेट

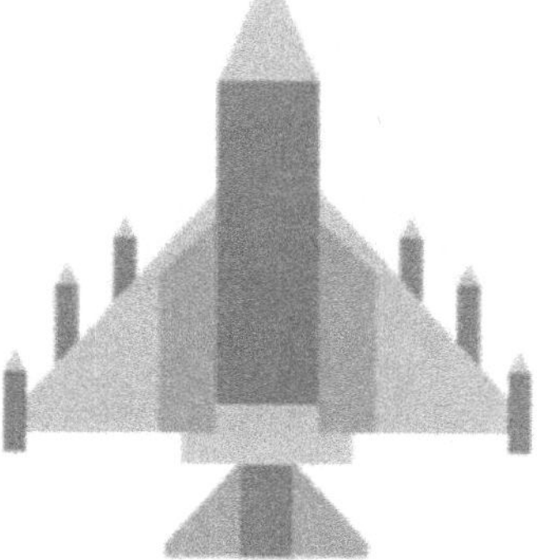

The jet is high-speed.

moto

मोटरसाइकिल

The motorcycle is on the road.

navire

समुंद्री जहाज

The ship is on the water.

métro

भूमिगत मार्ग

My mom goes on the subway to work.

taxi

टैक्सी

The taxi has someone inside.

train

रेल गाडी

The train is going slowly.

un camion

ट्रक

The truck has stuff in it.

asperges

एस्परैगस

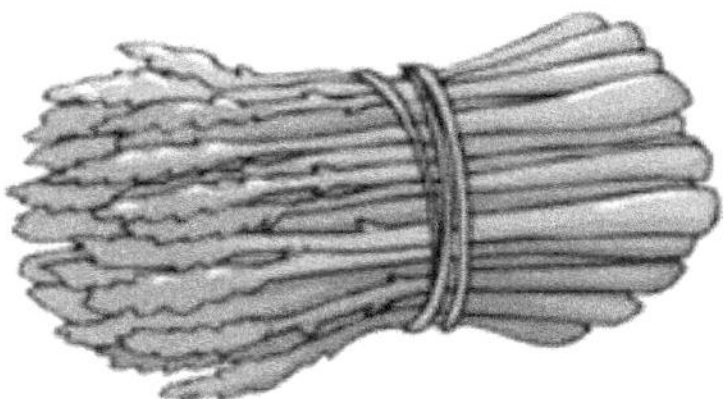

The asparagus is in a bundle.

des haricots

फलियां

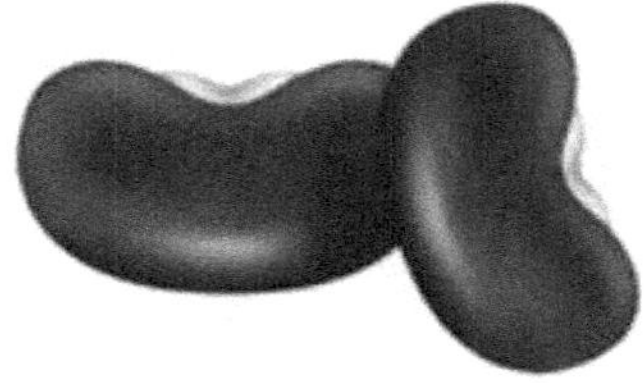

The beans are smooth.

brocoli

ब्रोकोली

The broccoli is dancing.

chou

पत्ता गोभी

Bunnies like to eat cabbage.

carotte

गाजर

The carrots are very long.

céleri

अजवायन

The celery has lots of leaves.

blé

मक्का

Corn soup is delicious.

concombre

खीरा

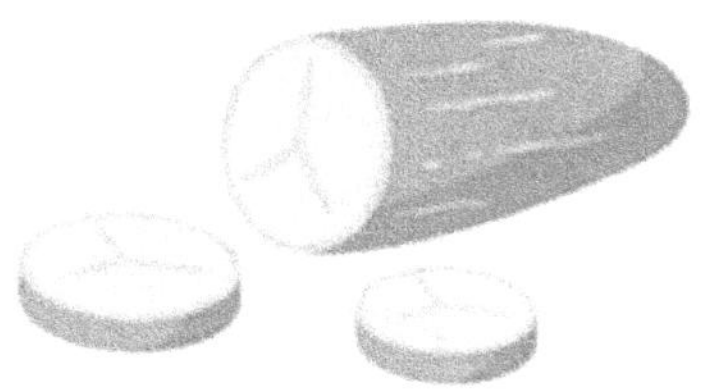

The cucumbers are cut into pieces.

aubergine

बैंगन

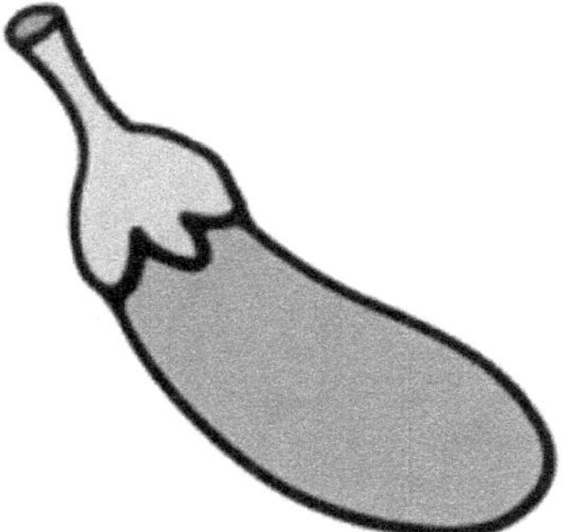

The eggplant is purple.

poivre vert

हरी मिर्च

The green pepper is juicy.

salade

सलाद

The lettuce is all green.

oignon

प्याज

The onions make my eyes water.

pois

मटर

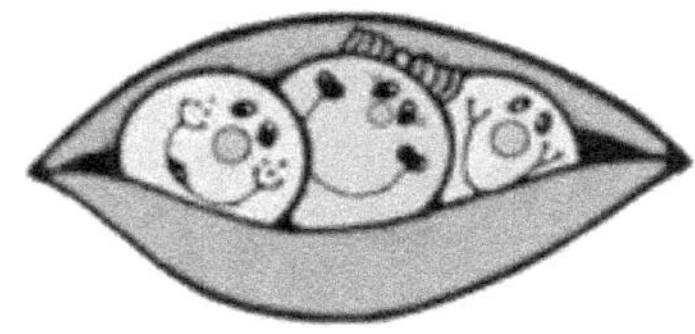

The peas are all in a pod.

patate

आलू

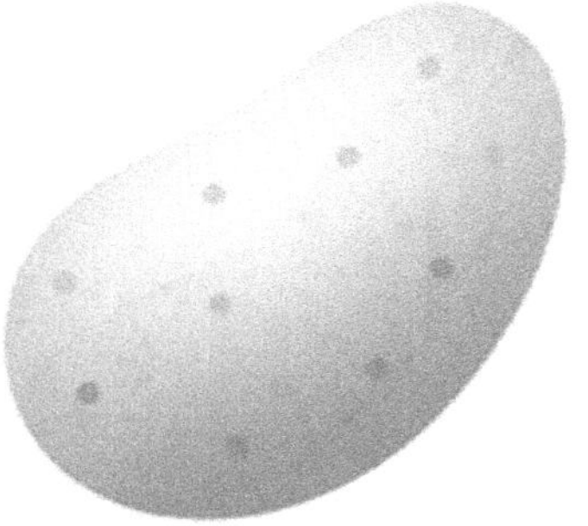

The potato is very shiny.

citrouille

कद्दू

The pumpkin is for Halloween.

un radis

मूली

The radish is a type of vegetable.

épinard

पालक

The spinach is good with cheese.

patate douce

शकरकंद

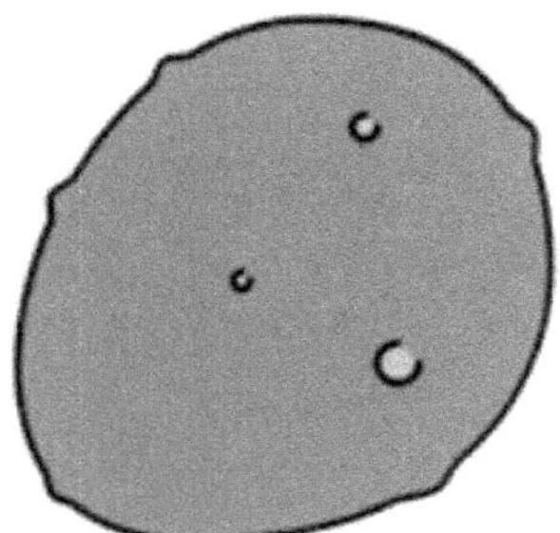

The sweet potato is quite sweet.

tomate

टमाटर

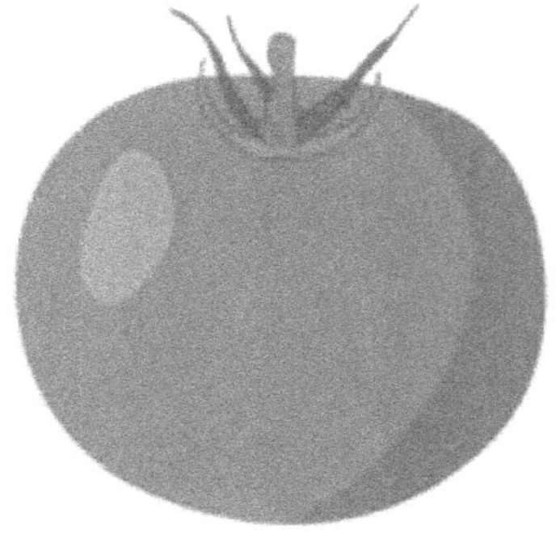

I don't like to eat tomatoes.

navet

शलजम

My mom bought some turnips.

nuageux

बादल

The weather is cloudy today.

du froid

सर्दी

I like cold weather.

cool

ठंडा

The temperature is cold today.

brumeux

धूमिल

The fog is so strong I can't see the city.

chaud

गरम

The fire is burning hot.

humide

नम

It's so humid and wet today.

pluvieux

बरसाती

It's raining very hard.

neigeux

हिमाच्छन्न

Welcome to snow land!

orageux

तूफ़ानी

I hate the stormy weather.

ensoleillé

धूप

The sun is shining!

chaud

गरम

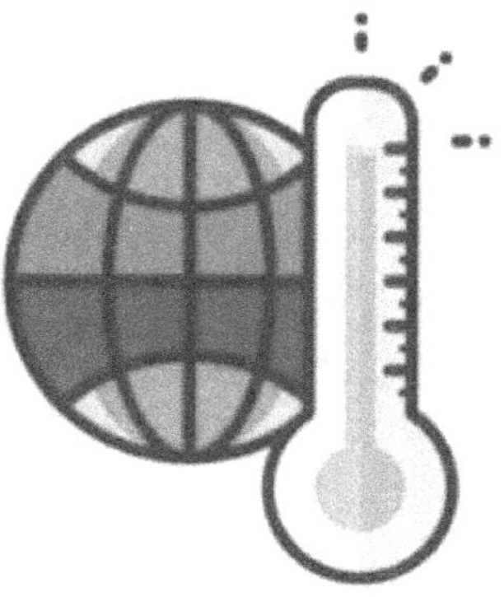

The whole world is warm today!

venteux

तूफानी

The leaves are blowing away since it's so windy!

tante

चाची

My aunt is very nice to me.

frère

भाई

My brother is very fun to play with.

cousin

चचेरा भाई

I love going to the playground with my cousin.

fille

बेटी

I like to read books with my daughter.

père

पिता जी

My father is playing with me.

petite fille

पोती

My granddaughter has blond hair.

grand-mère

दादी मा

My grandmother is very old and has glasses.

petit fils

पोता

My grandson and I are very excited today!

mère

मां

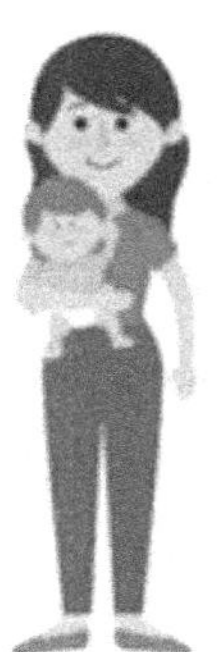

My mother likes to pick me up.

neveu

भतीजा

My father's nephew is my cousin.

nièce

भांजी

My niece is very good at playing ball.

sœur

बहन

My sister is so pretty!

fils

बेटा

My son likes to play with toy cars.

belle fille

सौतेली कन्या

My stepdaughter likes the color orange.

belle-mère

सौतेली माँ

My stepmother is pretty.

beau-fils

सौतेला बेटा

This is my stepson, Greg.

oncle

चाचा

My uncle tells lots of funny jokes.

bol

कटोरा

The bowl has nothing inside.

tasse

कप

My mom drinks her coffee out of a cup.

plat

थाली

That dish has a bone inside.

fourchette

कांटा

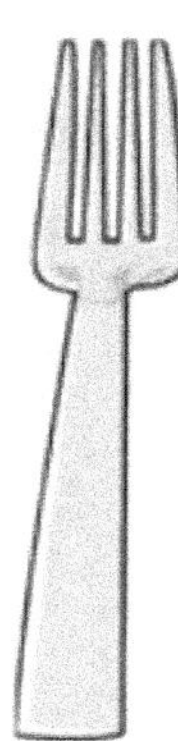

We have more spoons than forks.

verre

कांच

I have a glass of water on my desk.

couteau

चाकू

I have a knife in my kitchen.

agresser

मग

This mug of coffee is for my dad.

serviette de table

नैपकिन

You can use the napkins to clean your hands.

poivre

मिर्च

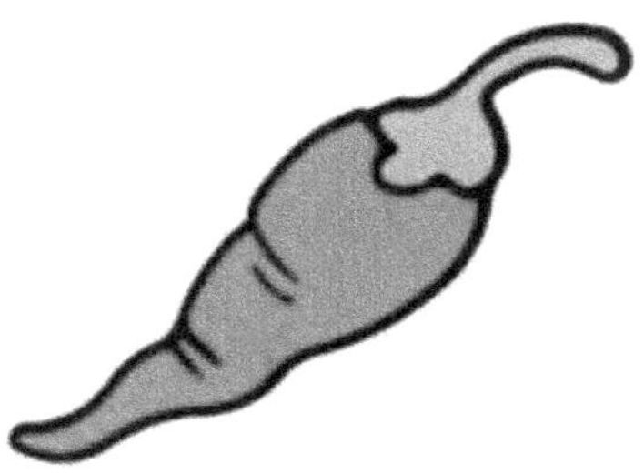

The pepper is very spicy.

lanceur

मटकी

Pour yourself some lemonade from the pitcher.

assiette

प्लेट

Can you help me wash the plates?

salade

सलाद

The salad is very healthy for you.

sel

नमक

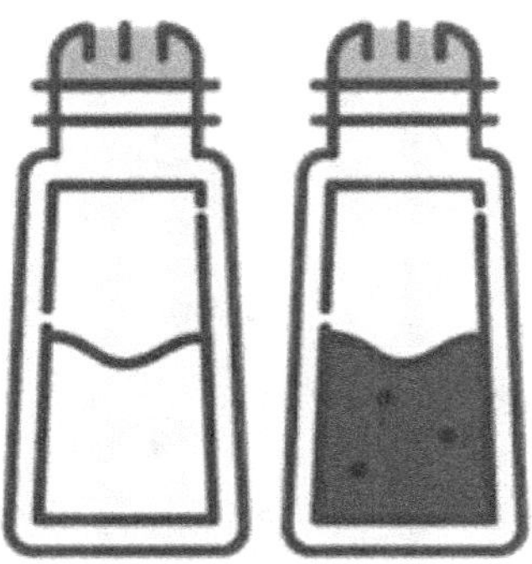

The salt tastes good with a few pinches of pepper.

soucoupe

तश्तरी

The plate is for my cup.

cuillère

चम्मच

I use a spoon to eat my rice.

sucre

चीनी

The pack of sugar is very heavy.

dimanche

रविवार

Sunday

Sunday is the day to go to Church!

lundi

सोमवार

Monday

Monday is the day to start school.

mardi

मंगलवार

Tuesday

We will go to the shops on Tuesday.

mercredi

बुधवार

Wednesday

Wednesday is hard to spell!

jeudi

गुरूवार

Thursday

Thursday is the fourth day of the week!

vendredi

शुक्रवार

Friday

My birthday is on Friday!

samedi

शनिवार

Saturday

Saturday is the weekend!

cuire

सेंकना

The chef will bake a cake.

ébullition

फोड़ा

I will boil the eggs.

griller

विवाद

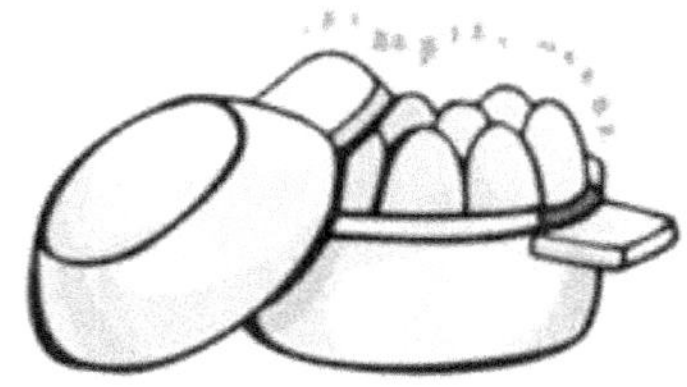

Broil is very yummy.

ouvre-boîte

कैन खोलने वाला

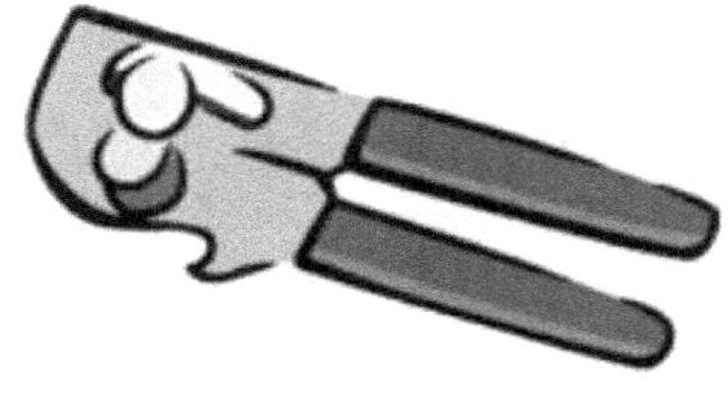

That can opener is used for opening cans.

frire

तलना

The pan can fry lots of things.

gril

ग्रिल

We have a grill in our backyard.

tasse à mesurer

मापने वाला कप

My mom uses the measuring cup for baking.

cuillère à mesurer

मापक चम्मच

I use a measuring spoon to eat my dessert.

four micro onde

माइक्रोवेव

The microwave is used to heat food.

bol à mélanger

मिश्रण का कटोरा

She is using the mixing bowl to mix things.

serviettes en papier

कागजी तौलिए

Dry your hands with paper towels.

poché aux œufs

अंडे का जूस

The poach is put on noodles.

porte pot

पॉट धारक

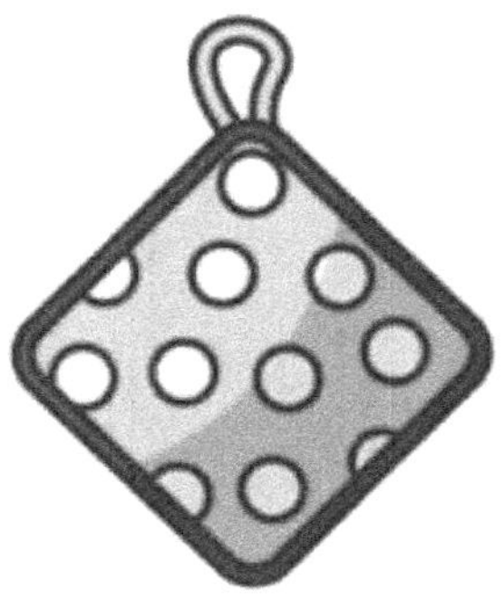

The potholder is soft.

rôti

भुना हुआ

The chef made roast chicken.

rouleau à pâtisserie

बेलन

He is holding a rolling pin.

brouiller

संघर्ष

My mom is making scrambled eggs for breakfast.

mijoter

उबाल

The simmer is rice today.

couteau

चाकू

The knife is sharp.

cuillère

चम्मच

I eat my food with a spoon and fork.

spatule

रंग

The spatula will help us flip the steak over.

vapeur

भाप

The steam is coming from the pot.

passoire

झरनी

The strainer is used to strain stuff.

minuteur

घड़ी

I set my timer for 12:00.

fourchette

कांटा

I have lots of metallic forks.

grille-pain

टोअस्टर

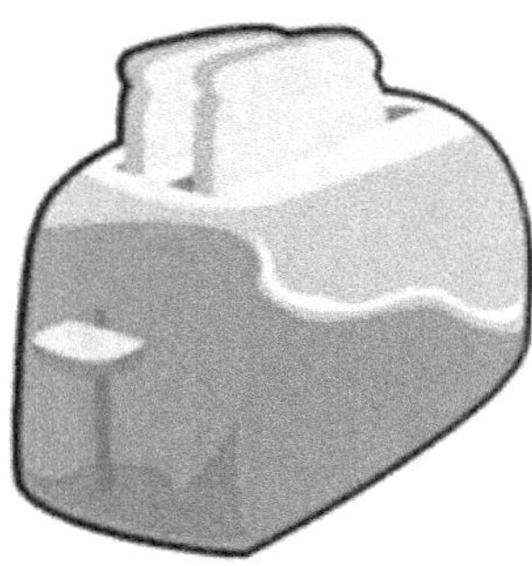

The toaster will toast my bread.

bouilloire

केतली

The kettle has tea inside.

réfrigérateur

फ्रिज

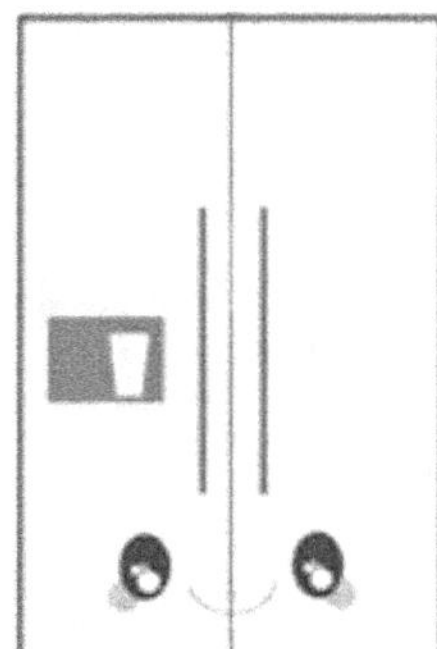

The refrigerator has lots of things inside.

mixeur

ब्लेंडर

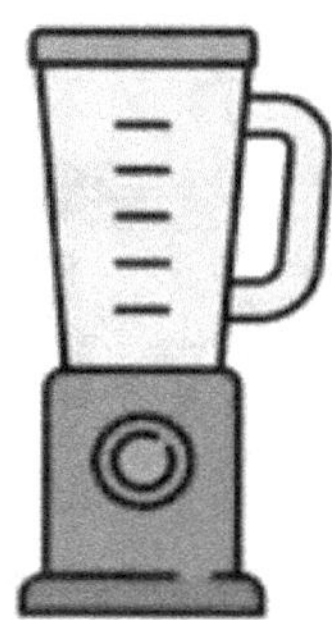

The blender will mix up my fruits.

cabinets

अलमारियाँ

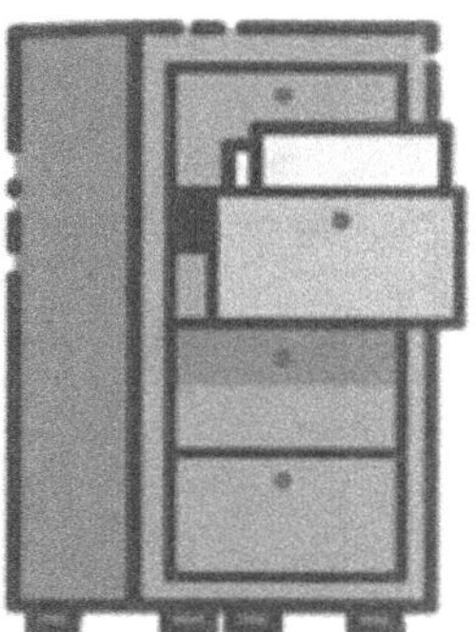

The cabinet has my paper inside.

placard

अलमारी

The cupboard has lots of books.

four micro onde

माइक्रोवेव

The microwave will heat my food.

arrière

वापस

She has a slender back.

des joues

गाल

She kisses her mom on the cheek.

poitrine

छाती

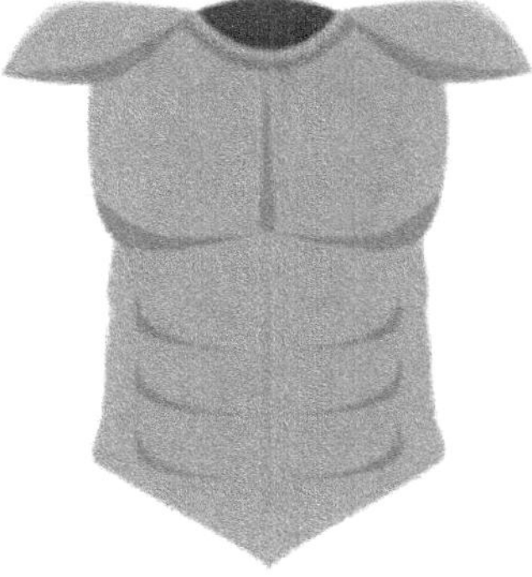

The armor is for your chest.

menton

ठोड़ी

This is my chin!

oreilles

कान

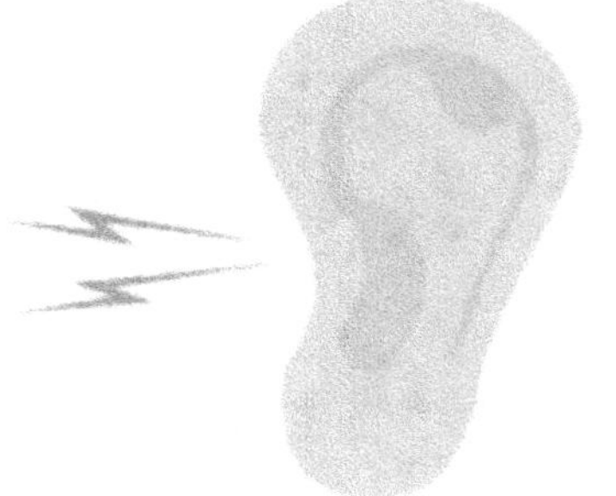

The ear is hearing something.

les sourcils

भौहें

The eyebrows are raised.

yeux

आंखें

The eyes are blue.

pieds

पैर का पंजा

I have one pair of feet.

des doigts

उंगलियों

The fingers are waving at us.

pied

पैर

My foot has five fingers.

front

माथा

My brain is behind my forehead.

cheveux

बाल

My hair is long and black.

mains

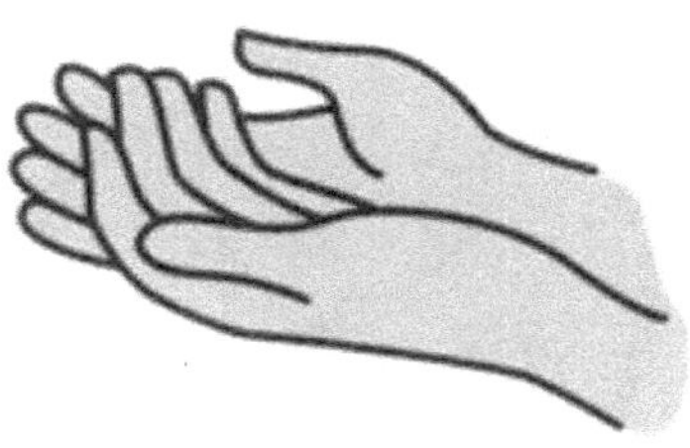

हाथ

I will wash my hands in the sink.

tête

सिर

She has a big head.

les hanches

कूल्हों

The gorilla has his hands on his hips.

les genoux

घुटने

She is begging on her knees.

jambes

पैर

The tiger has strong legs.

lèvres

होंठ

The lips have lipstick on.

bouche

मुंह

He is covering his mouth with his hand.

cou

गरदन

The necklace is very special to me.

nez

नाक

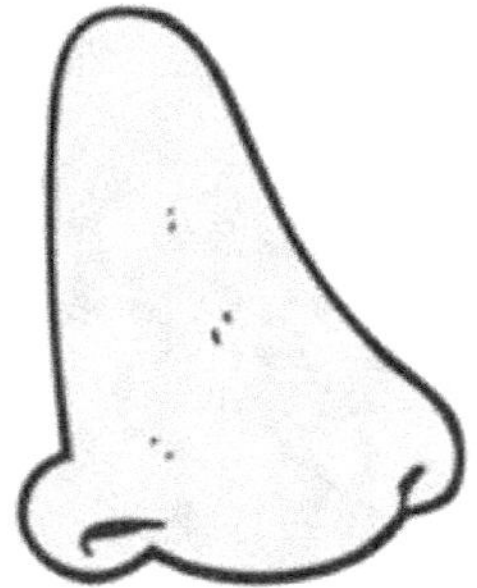

The nose smells something.

épaules

कंधों

He puts his hands on his shoulders.

estomac

पेट

He has a big stomach.

les dents

दांत

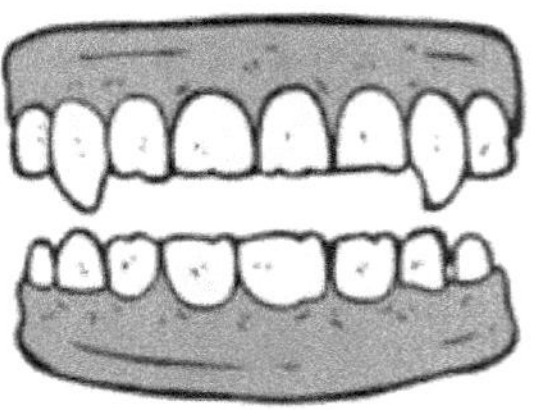

The teeth are clean and white.

gorge

गला

He has a sore throat today.

les orteils

पैर की उंगलियों

My toes are small.

langue

जुबान

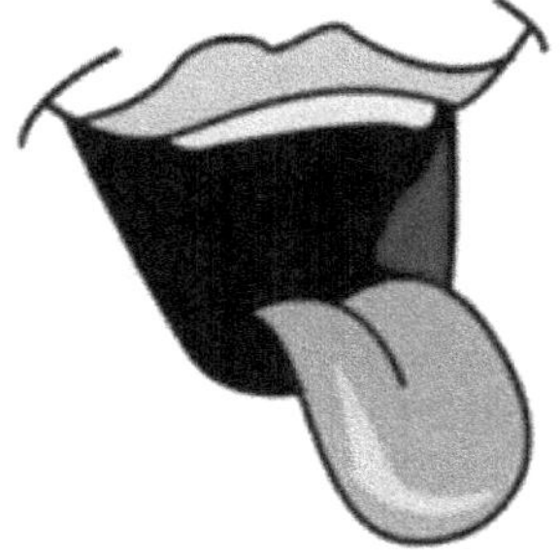

My tongue is licking ice cream.

dent

दांत

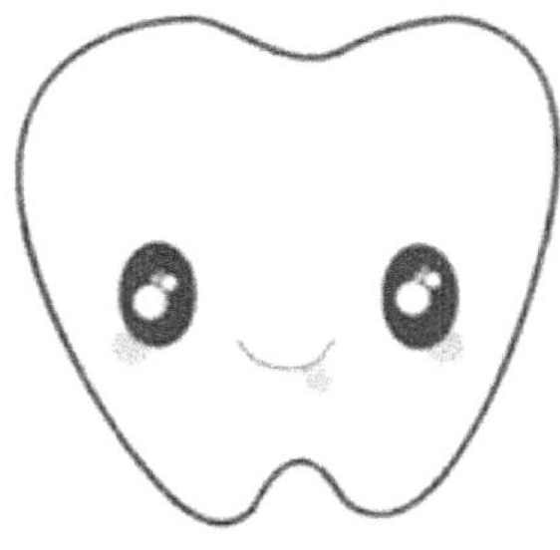

The tooth has big eyes.

taille

कमर

He has his hands on his waist.

salopette

चौगा

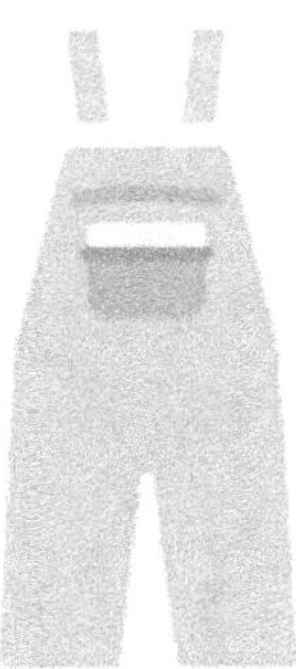

I bought these overalls for you!

mitaines

दस्ताने

The mittens are very warm.

bonnet

बेनी

The beanie is for winter.

tablier

तहबंद

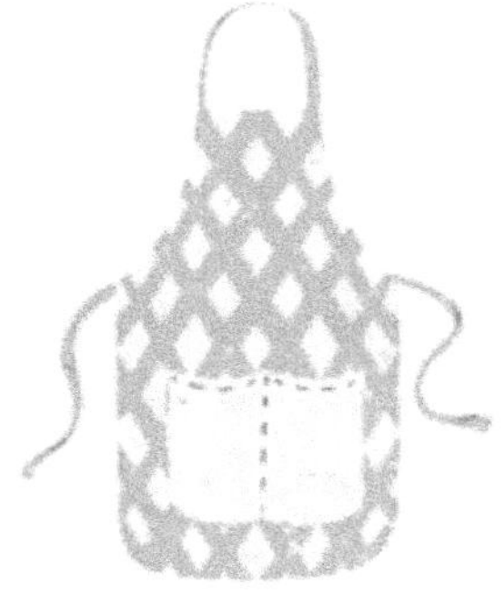

I wear my apron when I bake.

poupée

गुड़िया

The doll is for my baby sister.

hochets

झुनझुने

The rattle is for the baby.

jouet

खिलौना

The toy is very fun.

couche

डायपर

The baby has to wear a diaper.

berceau

बच्चों की गाड़ी

She is sleeping in her bassinet.

bavoir

अकसर पीना

My baby brother has to wear his
bib when he is eating.

octogone

अष्टकोना

The octagon is saying okay!

triangle

त्रिभुज

The triangle has three corners.

carré

वर्ग

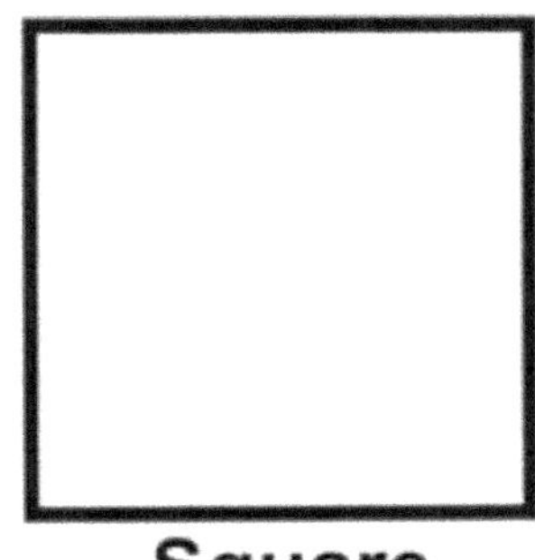

Square

The square has four sides.

cercle

वृत्त

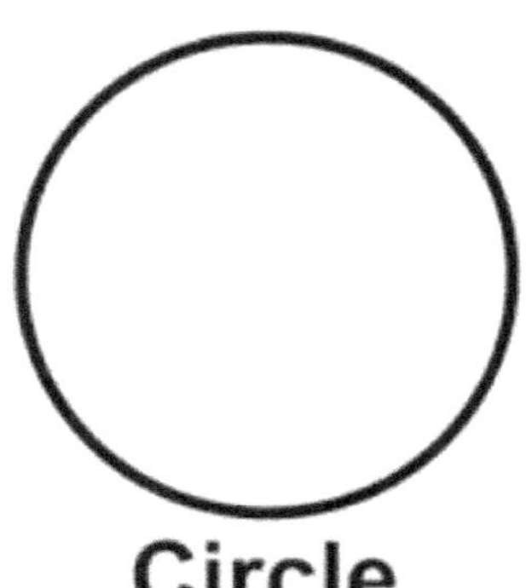

Circle

The circle is round.

ovale

अंडाकार

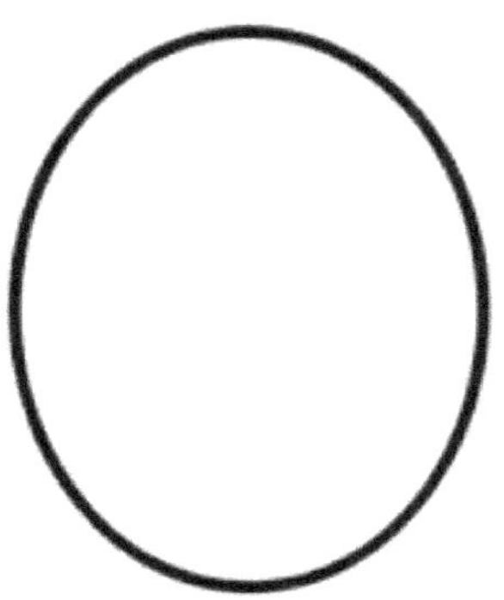

The oval shape looks like a circle.

cœur

दिल

I drew a heart on my paper.

traverser

पार करना

That sign is a cross.

la flèche

तीर

The arrow is pointing this way.

cube

घनक्षेत्र

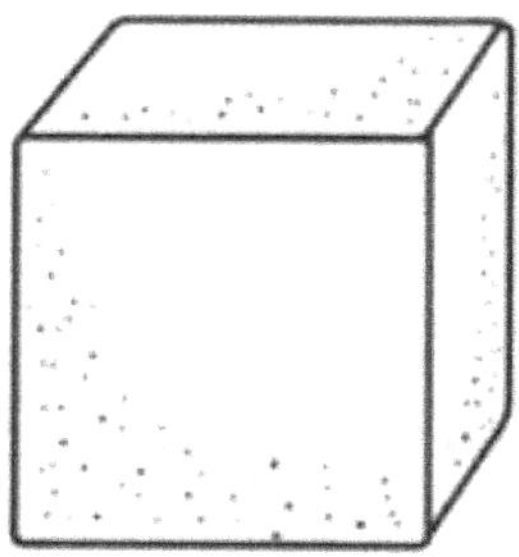

The cube is 3D.

étoile

सितारा

The star is yellow and shiny.

tir à l'arc

तीरंदाजी

The archery is where you aim.

badminton

बैडमिंटन

My favorite sport is badminton.

criquet

क्रिकेट

I am very good at cricket.

bowling

बॉलिंग

I got one pin down at bowling!

boxe

मुक्केबाज़ी

The boxing gloves are hot.

tennis

टेनिस

He can hit the ball in tennis.

faire de la planche a roulettes

स्केटबोर्डिंग

He skateboards to school.

planche de surf

surfboarding

The shark loves surfing in the ocean.

le hockey

हॉकी

I like to play Ice hockey.

yoga

योग

He is closing his eyes and doing yoga.

épée

तलवार का खेल

They are fencing and dueling together.

aptitude

स्वास्थ्य

She will do some fitness in the pool.

gymnastique

कसरत

He can do brilliant gymnastics.

karaté

कराटे

She is good at kicking in Karate.

volley-ball

वालीबाल

She is holding a volleyball.

musculation

भारोत्तोलन

The girl with brown hair can do weightlifting.

basketball

बास्केटबाल

He can balance the ball with one finger in basketball.

base-ball

बेसबॉल

The little chick is in the finales at baseball.

le rugby

रग्बी

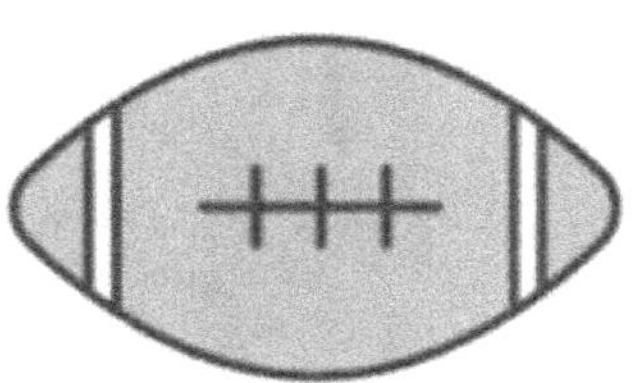

The rugby ball has white stripes.

lutte

कुश्ती

The sumo will compete in wrestling.

course de voitures

कार रेसिंग

He is number one for car racing.

cyclisme

सायक्लिंग

He is peacefully cycling on the road.

fonctionnement

चल रहा है

He is running while listening to his earphones.

tennis de table

टेबल टेनिस

My brother and dad will play table tennis.

pêche

मछली पकड़ना

He will go to the river to fish.

judo

जूदो

She has a red belt in Judo.

escalade

चढ़ना

He will climb the ladder.

tournage

शूटिंग

He is shooting the archery board.

le golf

गोल्फ़

She is going to compete in the golf competition.

balade

सवारी

He will ride his scooter.

asseyez-vous

बैठ जाओ

They are sitting down together.

se lever

खड़े हो जाओ

She likes to stand up.

bats toi

लड़ाई

They are fighting over the book.

rire

हसना

He is laughing so hard!

lis

पढ़ें

She read a picture book.

jouer

खेल

He went to play on the slide.

ecoutez

बात सुनो

He listened for the ice cream cart.

pleurer

रोना

He cried because he got a bad grade.

pense

सोच

He thought that the test would be hard.

chanter

गाओ

He sang for the concert.

regarder la télévision

टीवी देखो

He watched TV the whole night.

danse

नृत्य

She was a good dancer.

allumer

चालू करो

The light is turned on.

éteindre

बंद करें

The light is turned off.

gagner

जीत

He won the contest.

mouche

उड़ना

The parrot can fly.

couper

कट गया

He was cutting his nails.

désinvolte

फेंक देना

He threw away the garbage.

dormir

नींद

He slept soundly.

fermer

बंद करे

He closed his mouth shut.

ouvert

खुला हुआ

She opened the bathroom door.

écrire

लिखो

She wrote with a pencil.

donner

देना

Santa gave her a present.

sauter

कूद

She had fun jumping.

manger

खा

The shark ate yummy ice cream.

boisson

पीना

The old British man drank tea.

cuisinier

रसोइया

The microwave cooked his soup.

lavage

धुलाई

You need to remember to wash
your hands.

attendre

रुको

He was waiting for the bus.

montée

चढना

She climbed a lot of mountains.

parler

बातचीत

Two best friends were talking together.

crawl

क्रॉल

The baby crawled on the floor.

rêver

ख्वाब

The Sloth dreamed about eating leaves.

creuser

गड्ढा करना

That strong man dug a swimming pool.

taper

ताली

The baby clapped her hands.

tricoter

knit

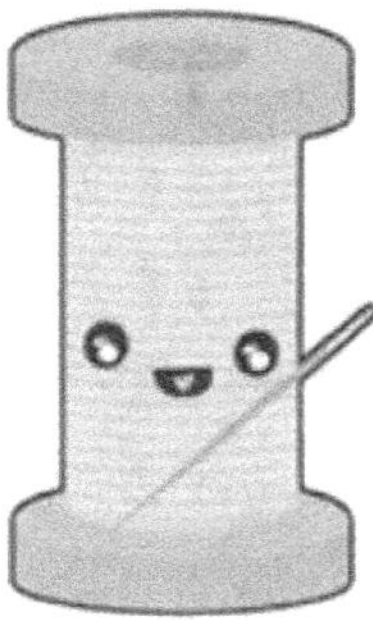

She knits with the purple string.

coudre

सिलना

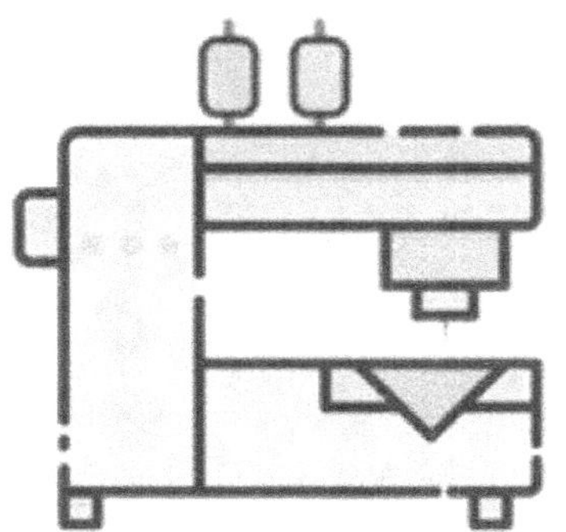

That is a sewing machine.

odeur

गंध

The perfume smelled great.

baiser

चुम्मा

He kissed his mother.

étreinte

झप्पी

They hugged each other.

ronfler

सोते सोते चूकना

The tiger snored.

baigner

स्नान

He took a bath.

s'incliner

झुकने

He bowed to the judge.

peindre

रंग

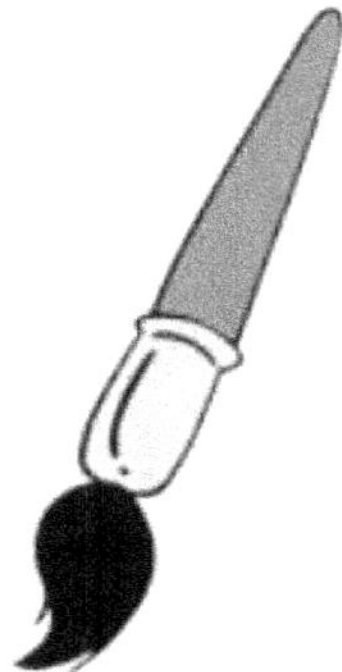

He painted a colorful picture.

se plonger

डुबकी

He dove to the deepest part of the ocean.

ski

स्की

The ski was expensive.

empiler

ढेर

The books are stacked high.

acheter

खरीदें

They bought cereal.

secouer

शेक

They shook hands together.

programmeur

प्रोग्रामर

He was a smart computer programmer.

vétérinaire

पशुचिकित्सा

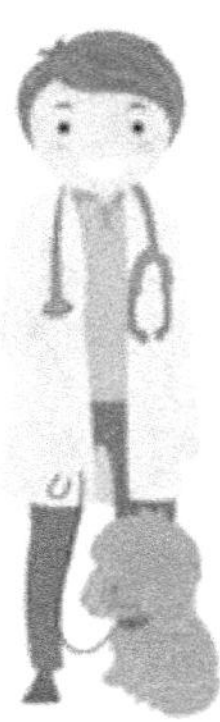

She is a veterinarian.

vendeur de rue

फेरीवाला

That street vendor sells hot dogs.

mineur

खान में काम करनेवाला

That Miner will find gold.

prof

अध्यापक

The owl is the teacher.

groom

नौकर

That Bellboy is fat.

orateur

वक्ता

The chicken is a great Speaker.

boucher

कसाई

The Butcher sells fish.

pharmacien

फार्मेसिस्ट

That Pharmacist saved a person's life.

réceptionniste

रिसेप्शनिस्ट

He is a Receptionist.

politicien

राजनीतिज्ञ

He wants to be a Politician.

guide touristique

टूर गाइड

That Tour guide led us around Japan.

entrepreneur

व्यवसायी

He is an Entrepreneur.

danseuse de ballet

बैले नृतकी

She is training to be a Ballet dancer.

astronaute

अंतरिक्ष यात्री

He is a great astronaut.

juge

न्यायाधीश

That Judge is always fair.

avocat

वकील

The lawyer is serious.

la caissière

केशियर

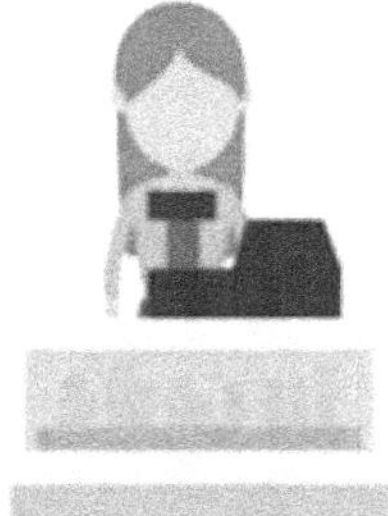

She is a cashier at the market.

conducteur de taxi

टैक्सी चलाने वाला

He is a fast Taxi driver.

plombier

नलसाज

That Plumber fixes toilets.

musicien

संगीतकार

She wants to be a Musician like her teacher.

chef

बावर्ची

The chef makes fast food.

boulanger

बेकर, नानबाई

That baker is a bread.

artiste

कलाकार

That Artist came from Italy.

acteur

अभिनेता

That actor is famous.

barman

भोजनशाला का नौकर

The Bartender works in a bar.

coiffeur

नाई

That girl is a Hairdresser.

évêques

बिशप

He is a Bishop.

opticien

प्रकाशविज्ञानशास्त्री

She went to an Optician.

fleuriste

फूलवाला

She is a great Florist.

écrivain

लेखक

He is a famous author.

comptable

मुनीम

My accountant is loyal.

du vin

वाइन

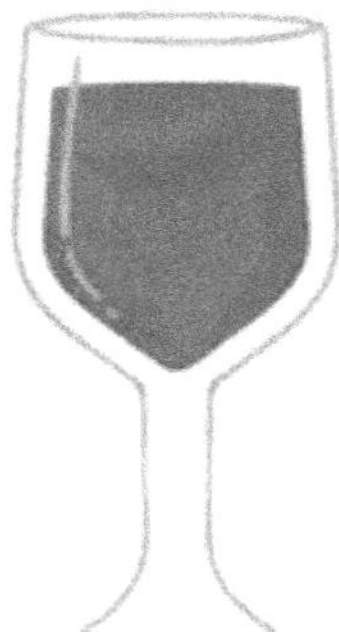

That wine tastes good.

café

कॉफ़ी

That coffee is bitter.

limonade

नींबु पानी

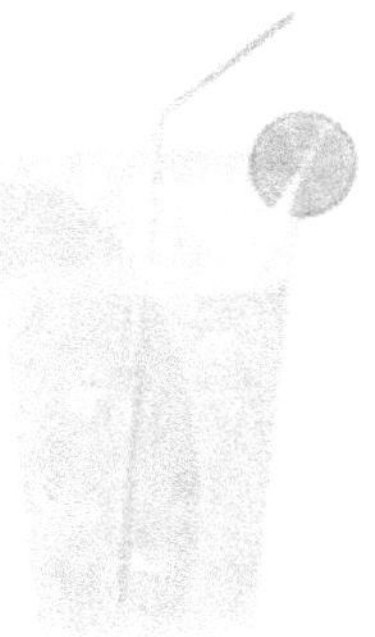

The lemonade is refreshing.

chocolat chaud

गर्म चॉकलेट

I drink hot chocolate every day.

milk-shake

मिल्कशेक

The milkshake has whipped cream.

eau

पानी

The water is not cold.

thé

चाय

The tea is hot.

lait

दूध

Milk is white.

bière

बीयर

The beer is foamy.

un soda

सोडा

The soda is fizzy.

smoothie

ठग

The smoothie is a watermelon flavor.

milk-shake

मिल्कशेक

The milkshake has whipped cream.

lait de coco

नारियल का दूध

The coconut milk is yummy.

du jus d'orange

संतरे का रस

The orange juice is made from oranges.

cacao

कोको

The cocoa is sweet.

fromage

पनीर

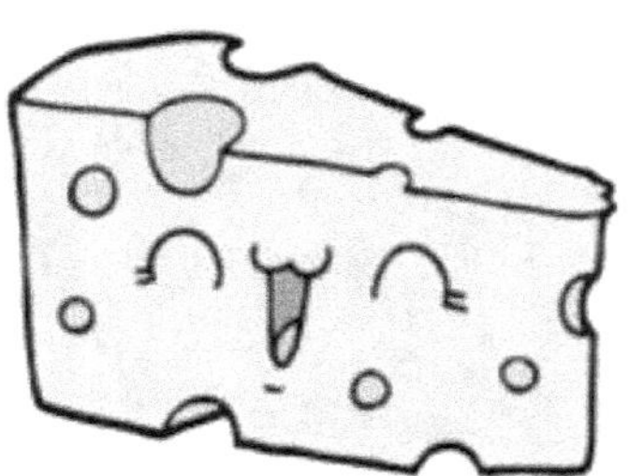

The cheese is creamy.

oeuf

अंडा

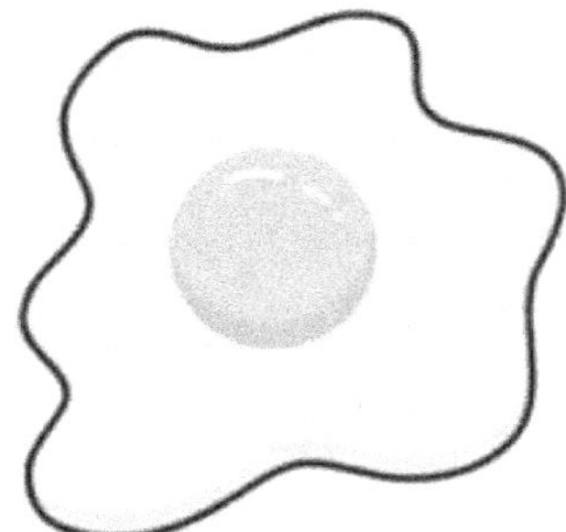

The egg is fried.

beurre

मक्खन

The butter is put on bread.

margarine

नकली मक्खन

Margarine looks like butter.

yaourt

दही

That yogurt is popular.

cottage cheese

छाना

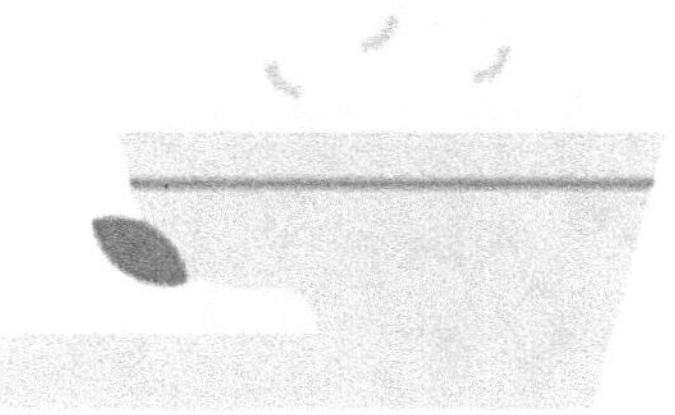

The cottage cheese is put on crackers.

crème glacée

आइसक्रीम

They have a triple scoop ice cream.

crème

मलाई

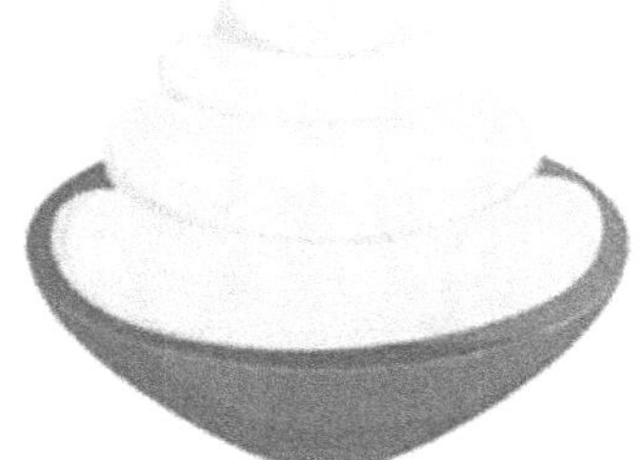

That is a lot of creams.

sandwich

सैंडविच

That sandwich is healthy.

saucisse

सॉस

Americans love sausages.

hamburger

हैमबर्गर

That hamburger looks happy.

hot-dog

हॉट - डॉग

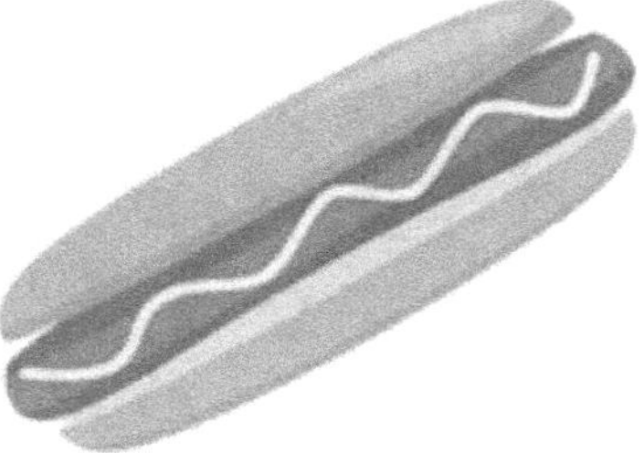

That hot dog has mustard on it.

pain

रोटी

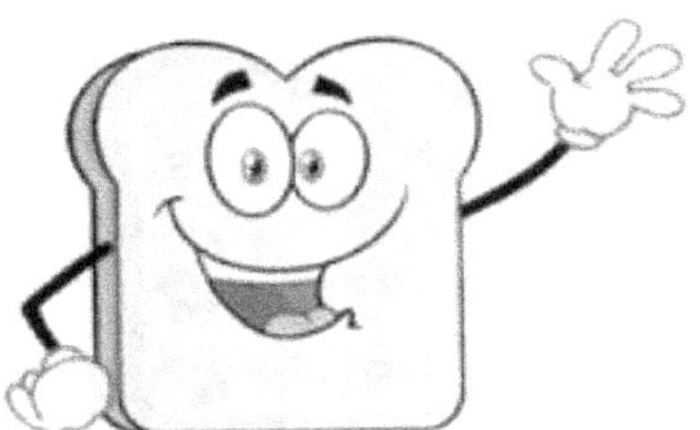

That bread is saying hello.

pizza

पिज़्ज़ा

That pizza is cheesy.

steak

स्टेक

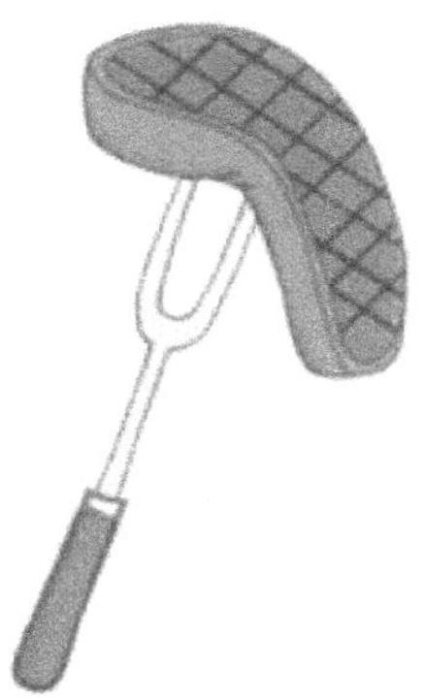

The steak was grilled.

poulet rôti

भुना हुआ मुर्ग

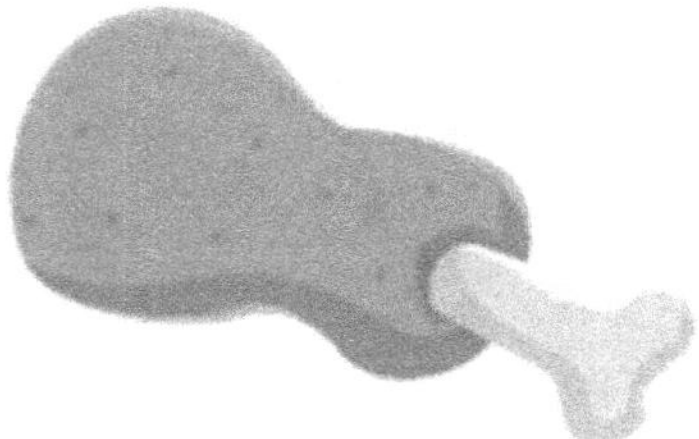

Roast Chicken is delicious.

poisson

मछली

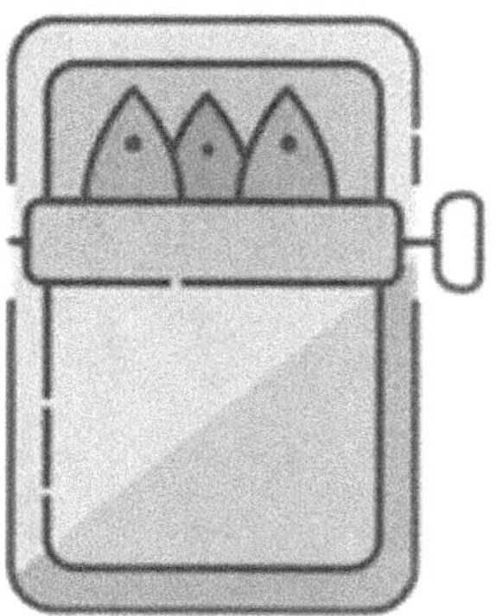

You can buy canned fish in the market.

fruit de mer

समुद्री भोजन

Lobster is expensive seafood.

jambon

जांघ

Ham can be put in sandwiches.

kebab

कबाब

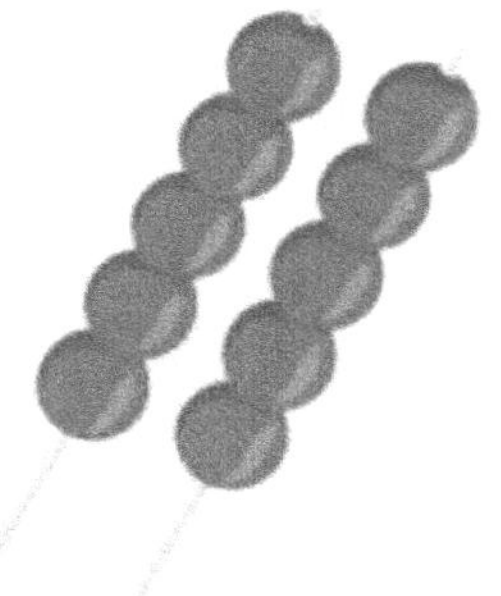

Kebab is a delicacy in America.

bacon

सूअर का मांस

That bacon is smiling.

crème fraîche

खट्टी मलाई

You can dip your chips in sour cream.

vache

गाय

Cows are black and white.

lapin

खरगोश

That rabbit is fun to play with.

canard

बत्तख

That duck is content.

crevette

झींगा

The shrimp has six legs.

porc

सूअर

That pig is pink and fat.

abeille

मधुमक्खी

The bee has a stinger.

chèvre

बकरा

That goat has a white horn.

crabe

केकड़ा

The crab has two big pincers.

cerf

हिरन

That deer is sleeping.

dinde

तुर्की

The turkey has a giant tail.

colombe

डव

That dove is carrying a plant.

mouton

भेड़

That sheep has fluffy wool.

poisson

मछली

That fish has colorful fins.

poulet

मुर्गी

That chicken is waking everybody up.

cheval

घोड़ा

The horse has a red mane.

chaise

कुरसी

That wing chair is yellow.

meuble tv

टीवी स्टैंड

The TV stand can hold books.

canapé

सोफ़ा

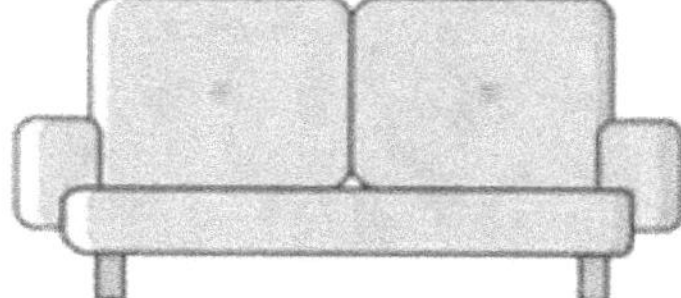

The sofa is comfortable to sit on.

coussins

कुशन

The cushion helps soften your seat.

téléphone

टेलीफोन

The telephone is ringing.

télévision

टेलीविजन

That television is big.

haut-parleurs

वक्ताओं

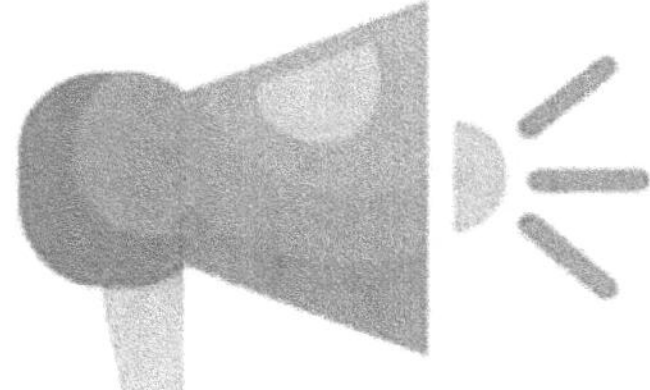

That speaker is used to increase the volume.

table d'appoint

बगल की मेज

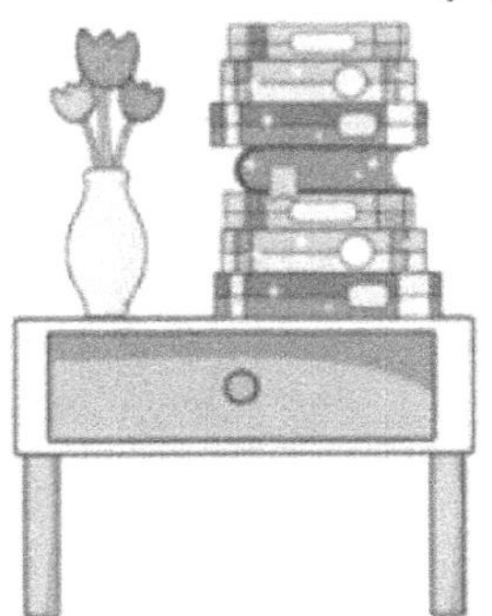

That end table is sparkling clean.

service à thé

चाय का सेट

That tea set is from China.

cheminée

चिमनी

The fireplace makes me warm.

télécommandes

दूरस्थ

The remote has lots of buttons.

ventilateur électrique

बिजली का पंखा

The fan is blowing wind.

lampadaire

जमीन पर रखा जाने वाला लैंप

The floor lamp is very tall.

tapis

गलीचा

The carpet is soft and silky.

bureaux

डेस्क

The table is made of wood.

stores

ब्लाइंड

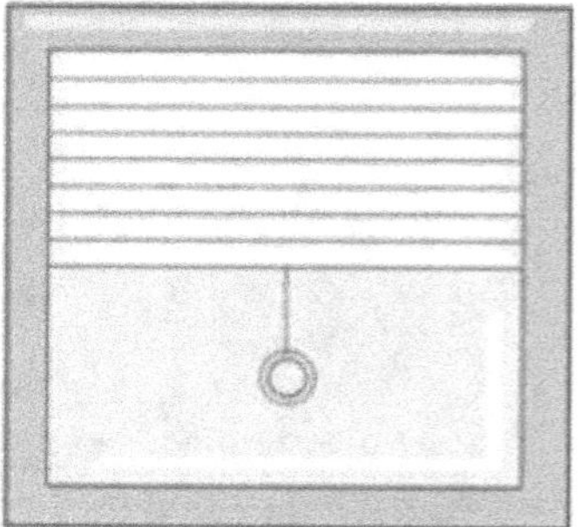

I will pull the blinds down.

rideaux

पर्दे

She opened the curtains.

image

चित्र

The picture is about the mountains and the sky.

vase

फूलदान

The roses are all in a vase.

l'horloge

घड़ी

The alarm clock is beeping.

oreiller

तकिया

The pillow is pink and yellow.

cintre

हैट हैंगर

The hat stand has only one hat on it.

mettre la table

श्रृंगार - पटल

I have made up on my dressing table.

lampe de table

टेबल लैंप

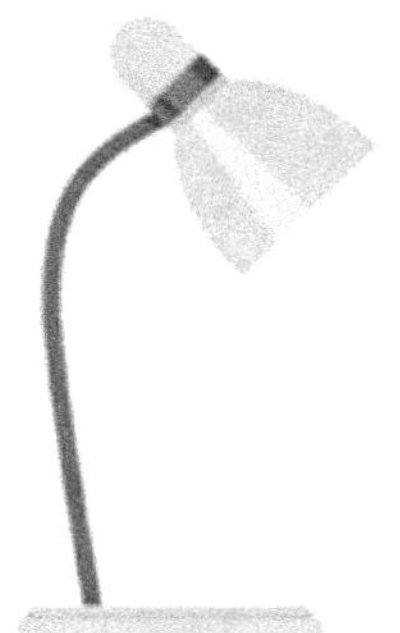

The table lamp will help me see in the dark.

miroir

आईना

The mirror is very tall.

planche a repasser

इस्त्री करने का बोर्ड

Don't touch the ironing board, it's hot!

boîte avec tiroir

दराज के साथ बॉक्स

You can keep your clothes in the hope chest.

table de chevet

बेड के बगल रखी जाने वाली मेज

The nightstand has my lamp on it.

lit

बिस्तर

The bed is charming.

climatisation

एयर कंडीशनर

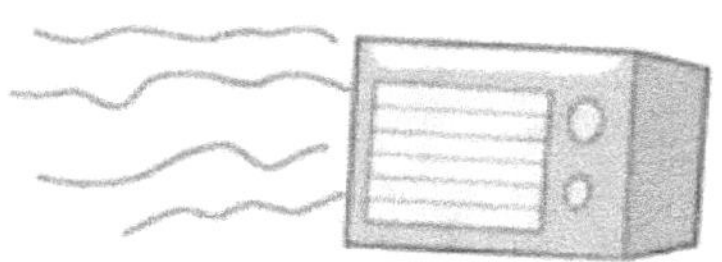

The air conditioner is cold.

cruche

सुराही

The measuring jug has nothing inside.

dentifrice

टूथपेस्ट

The toothpaste is mint flavored.

brosse à dents

टूथब्रश

The toothbrush has toothpaste on it.

savon

साबुन

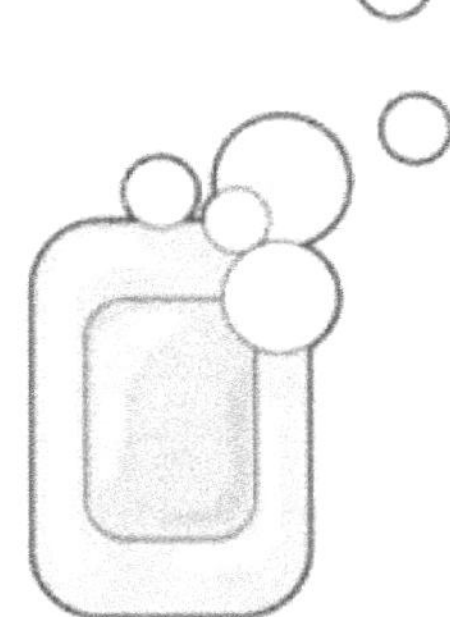

The soap is very bubbly.

pince à linge

clothespin के

The clothespin will clip my clothes.

cintre

कांटा

The hanger is hanging my boots.

sèche-cheveux

हेयर ड्रायर

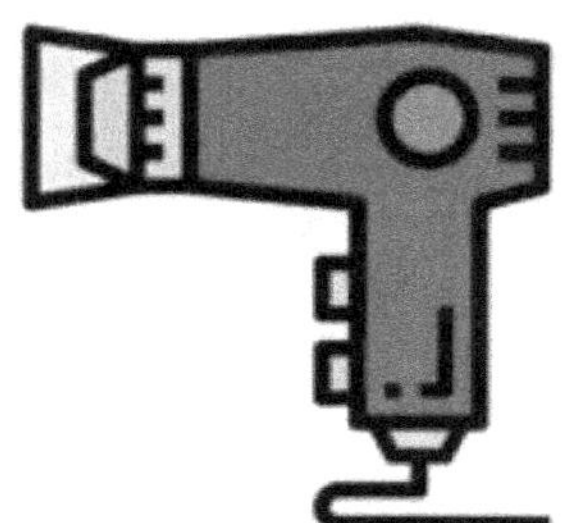

The hairdryer will blow my hair.

shampooing

शैम्पू

The shampoo is used to clean your hair.

bulle

बुलबुला

The bubbles are very fun to play in.

brosse

ब्रश

She is brushing her hair with the brush.

papier toilette

टॉयलेट पेपर

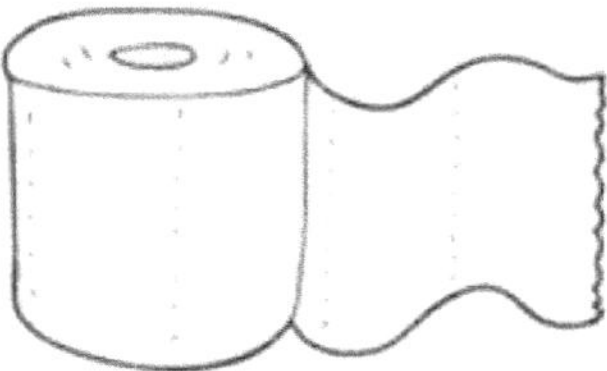

The toilet paper is used to dry your hands.

serviette

तौलिया

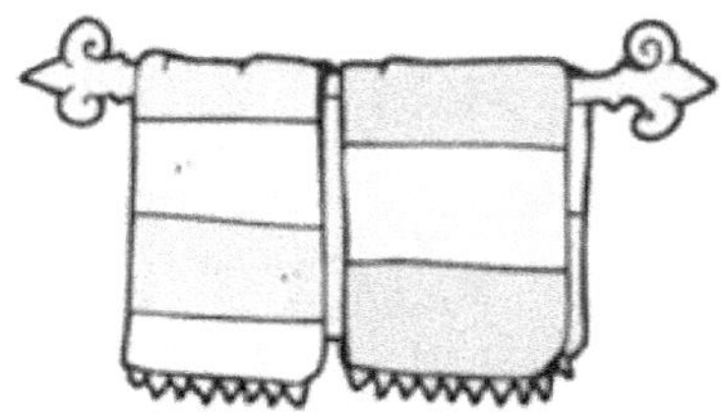

We have two towels on the rack.

corde à linge

क्लोथ्सलाइन

My shirt is hanging on the clothesline.

douche

शावर

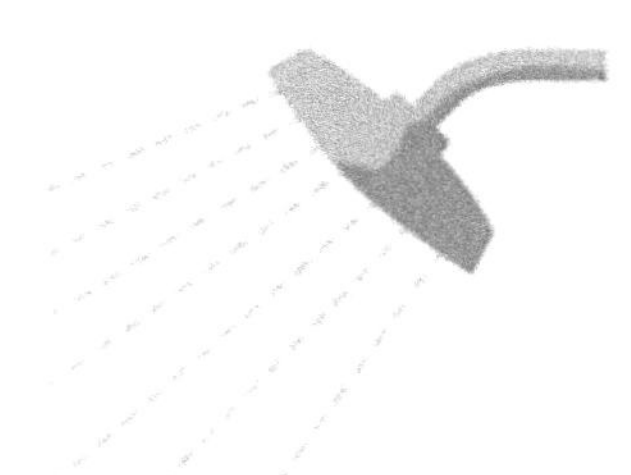

The shower is spraying water.

baignoire

बाथटब

The bathtub is comfortable.

lessive

कपड़े धोने का साबुन

The laundry detergent is used with the washing machine.

seau

बाल्टी

Can you help me fill up the bucket?

vadrouilles

मॉप

The mop is used for mopping the floor.

savon liquide

तरल साबुन

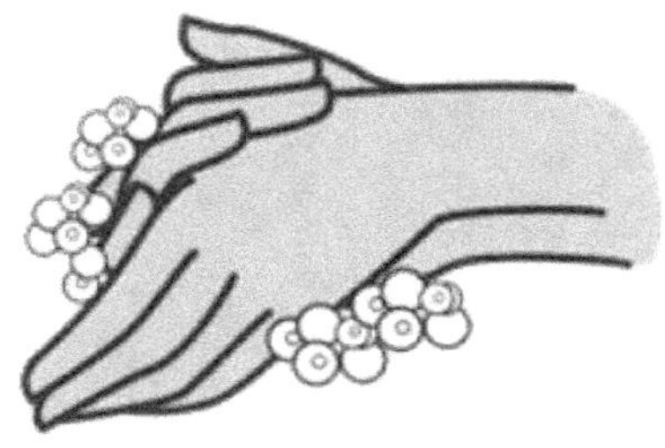

I use soapy water to wash my hands.

lessive en poudre

कपड़े धोने का पाउडर

I will scoop up the washing powder.

sac poubelle

कचरा बैग

The trash bag is full of trash.

poubelle

कचरे का डब्बा

You have only to put recylcle trash in the trash can.

les puits

सिंक

You should wash your hands in the sink.

cuvette des toilettes

शौचालय का कटोरा

She let her bunny use the toilet.

machine à laver

वॉशिंग मशीन

The washing machine wash your clothes.

panier à linge

कपड़े धोने की टोकरी

She is putting all the clothes into the laundry basket.

le rasoir

उस्तरा

He uses the razor to shave his beard.

rasoir électrique

विद्युत उस्तरा

The electric razor works faster than the normal one.

crème à raser

शेविंग क्रीम

The shaving cream is fluffy.

bain de bouche

mouthwash

The mouthwash smells very lovely.

coton-tige

रुई की कली

Q-tip can be used for many things.

brosse à cheveux

बाल ब्रश

She brushes her hair with her hairbrush.

peigne

कंघी

Her dad will comb her hair for her.

nettoyant

cleanser

Put the cap back on the cleanser bottle.

échelle

स्केल

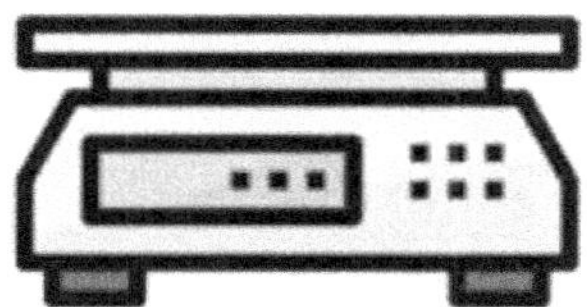

You can measure things on the scale.

papier de soie

महीन काग़ज़

The tissue is on the counter.

jouets de bain

स्नान खिलौने

The little duck is a bath toy.

robinet

नल

The faucet is broken.

miroir

आईना

He is looking in the mirror.

tapis de bain

स्नानघर का गलीचा

The bath mat is purple and yellow.